D0407763

BY THE SAME AUTHOR

The Book of Heroic Failures

CANNIBALS IN THE CAFETERIA

And Other Fabulous Failures

Stephen Pile

with Cartoons by Larry

1817

Harper & Row, Publishers, New York

Grand Rapids, Philadelphia, St. Louis, San Francisco
London, Singapore, Sydney, Tokyo, Toronto

The excerpt from "Rocks Off" (Jagger/Richard) © 1972 is reproduced by permission of EMI Music Publishing Ltd., London WC2H 0LD.

This book was previously published in 1988 in Great Britain by Martin Secker & Warburg Limited under the title *The Return of Heroic Failures*. It is here reprinted by arrangement with Martin Secker & Warburg Limited.

CANNIBALS IN THE CAFETERIA. Copyright © 1988 by Stephen Pile. Cartoons copyright © 1988 by Larry. All rights reserved. Printed in the United States of America. No part of this book may be used or reproduced in any manner whatsoever without written permission except in the case of brief quotations embodied in critical articles and reviews. For information address Harper & Row, Publishers, Inc., 10 East 53rd Street, New York, N.Y. 10022.

FIRST U.S. EDITION

LIBRARY OF CONGRESS CATALOG CARD NUMBER 89-45794
ISBN 0-06-016283-X

90 91 92 93 94 HC 10 9 8 7 6 5 4 3 2 1

To Quin Xiang-Yi
who in 1846 was given the title
'distinguished failure' in recognition
of his 20 years spent failing the
Chinese Civil Service entrance exams.
Buoyed up by this honour, he went
on to fail several times more.

CONTENTS

CONTENTS

ACKNOWLEDGEMENTS

I would like to thank Mark Mills and Jane Walker for their invaluable help with research; Bill Addis for bravely advising on the perils of new technology and for reading the manuscript when he had much more important things to do and for making countless helpful suggestions; the Fergusons of Tenby and Etha B. Fox of Chicago who spot things I miss; my mother and my brother Rob for all their help; and Siân for everything.

ACKNOWLEDGMENTS

INTRODUCTION

Friends, Romans and fellow incompetents, hello again.

You have all by now lost your copies of *The Book of Heroic Failures* and some of you have gone to even greater lengths and not read it at all. Perhaps I should start by reminding everyone that it was a heartfelt counterblast to the all-pervading success ethic in Western culture.

Success is overrated and Man's real genius lies in quite the opposite direction. Being really bad at something requires skill, panache, style and utter individualism. That book sang the praises of the worst in every sphere, people who were so bad at their chosen endeavour that their names shine like beacons for future generations.

At the time, none of us dreamed that there could ever be a second volume. Humanity had surely reached the frontiers of what was possible in our field.

Could anyone hope to match the immortal Nuttall, an explorer with no sense of direction whatsoever who was perpetually lost? His colleagues had to light fires at night so he could find his way back to the camp.

Could anyone surpass the world's worst tourist, Mr Nicholas Scotti, who spent two days in New York thinking he was in Rome?

Would anybody ever break the record for the smallest audience for a live theatrical show (one)?

The answer, we now know, is: yes. *Homo sapiens* has moved onwards and downwards to ever more glorious feats.

Indeed, we have just lived through a golden age. Connoisseurs among you will know, for example, that 1980 was a vintage year. It brought an incredible outburst of achievement to admire and savour. It warrants a whole chapter of its own.

Elsewhere, it has been a decade of solid achievement. The cultural sphere has seen amazing creativity while the criminal mind has once again surpassed itself with a consistently high level of performance.

We must also applaud the huge growth of activity in the United States of America, which lagged behind for so many years, but has now shot ahead, with more entries than any other part of the world. Given its size and tremendous natural resources, there is no reason why this still-young country should not lead the field in time and make a genuine contribution to our subject. The Soviet Union has also made its first entry with the least successful wedding toast on record.

But there have been disappointments too. The political sphere has been sluggish and I have regrettably been obliged to close down that entire chapter. Must try harder.

I, too, have been something of a disappointment in the past ten years, never quite fulfilling that youthful promise when my skills ranged freely across musical, sporting, academic and so many other fields. I can point with genuine pride to only one significant achievement in this entire period.

In a moment of weakness the British Broadcasting Corporation asked me to chair a new radio quiz. A pilot version was made of a rather complex game, the rules of which I did not, fortunately, begin to understand. I said 'Well, good evening' at the start of the programme and 'Well, good night' at the end. Between these pronouncements, however, I remained largely silent while chaos and confusion reigned.

On hearing this taped recording one member of the selection committee was kind enough to say that I was the worst quiz chairman in the history of the light entertainment department, which was most gratifying. Others did not realize that the programme had a chairman at all. The committee, however, united in the progressive, heartening and utterly correct view that this show should be abandoned immediately.

Also, I am pleased to report that *The Book of Heroic Failures* was a terrific flop in America, where sales took ages to reach double figures. Furthermore, readers will be glad to hear that the American edition came out with an erratum slip which was longer than the one listed in the book as a world record. (They omitted a healthy chunk of the introduction, an improvement which added a much-needed air of mystery to the work.)

When the Taiwan pirate edition came out, they knew nothing of this erratum slip with the result that their excellent version began 'And so in 1976.'

THE NOT TERRIBLY GOOD CLUB OF GREAT BRITAIN

Formed in 1977, with myself as president, the Not Terribly Good Club of Great Britain was a gathering of people from all walks of incompetence. Our heart-warming meetings included an exhibition of our art, Salon Des Incompetents, and a regatta with only one air-bed, which made the races less hotly competitive than is customary on these occasions.

The first volume was designed as the club's official handbook. When it appeared in a best-seller list I was thrown out as president, having brought shame upon the membership.

In only a few months the club had received 20,000 enquiries from members of the public wishing to join. And so in 1979 the club disbanded on the grounds that it was now a roaring success. Even as failures, we failed.

Since then I have been lying low and saying little on the subject. But my passion for it has continued unabated. I surface now to celebrate the tenth anniversary of *The Book of Heroic Failures* and to show that there is no limit to what humanity can achieve.

ONE

NEW WORLD RECORDS

In which Hamlet gets stuck to a Morris
Minor; Mrs Hitchens builds a garage; and
modern technology shows the Vatican in
a new light.

THE SMALLEST AUDIENCE

In August 1980 Joan Melu, a Rumanian folk singer broke all existing records for the smallest-ever audience. Effortlessly pushing aside the previous contenders he drew an audience of none whatsoever for a concert of what he described as his own style of country and western.

Arriving on stage at the Capitol Theatre, Melbourne, in dark glasses and casual clothing, he gazed down on 2,200 empty seats and gave a two-hour show which overran by thirty minutes due to encores.

Mr Melu performed throughout as if people were there. Coming back on stage after a fifteen-minute interval, the singer announced over the speaker system: 'Ladies and gentlemen, Joan Melu.' Towards the end of the performance he asked: 'Hey everybody, do you want to hear my new one?'

After the show he said that he was 'a little nervous' beforehand, but felt very satisfied with the way it had gone. 'I love this life,' the artist commented.

According to a stagehand, Mr Melu perched on a stool one metre from the edge of the stage and did not move for two hours except to strum his guitar without any attempt at chords and to mumble into the microphone in a monotone fashion. 'Every song appeared the same, musically and vocally.'

Faced with this criticism, the singer said that he doesn't pay too much attention to the music because 'life is in the song not the notes'.

OXFORD AND CAMBRIDGE BOAT RACE: LATEST

Cambridge have shot into the lead in the boat race. In 1983 the crews were level, having each sunk three times. (Cambridge showed the way in 1857 and 1978, but valiant Oxford saved their face in 1925 and 1981.)

But then in 1984 pioneering Cambridge achieved the unique distinction of sinking before the race began. Twenty minutes from the start they rowed into a moored tug and split their own boat in half.

Full of admiration, the race umpire, Mr Michael Sweeney, observed, 'The cox is only small and he is sitting behind big men. He must have been unsighted.'

For sheer style this rivals the great 1912 race in which both boats sank. Oxford went under first and made for the bank. Once the boat had been emptied of water, they could not restart because a brilliant oarsman had disappeared into the crowd to chat with a friend. Some while later he returned and told his disbelieving crew mates that it was 'my chum Boswell'.

Oxford then saw Cambridge go by, but they were swimming and their boat was nowhere visible. Sadly, this fine race was abandoned just as it was getting interesting.

THE FASTEST FAILURE OF A DRIVING TEST

Until recently the world record was held by Mrs Helen Ireland of Auburn, California, who failed her driving test in the first second, cleverly mistaking the accelerator for the clutch and shooting straight through the wall of the Driving Test Centre.

This seemed unbeatable until 1981 when a Lanarkshire motor mechanic called Thomson failed the test before the examiner had even got into the car. Arriving at the test centre he tooted the horn to summon the examiner, who strode out to the vehicle, said it was illegal to sound your horn while stationary, announced that Thomson had failed and strode back in again. Genius of this kind cannot be taught. It is a natural gift.

THE MOST DIVORCED MAN

Upon few men do the eternal bonds of holy matrimony have less of a grip than Glynn de Moss 'Scotty' Wolfe. When we last heard of him he was just divorcing wife number 23 on the grounds that she used his toothbrush. By 1986 he had set a new world record of 26 divorces.

A former marriage guidance counsellor, he says that 'everyone should get married. I always have been. Only the faces change'.

Now eighty, he claims to remember the names of practically all his wives. 'Helen, was first in 1931,' he said. 'Then followed in rapid succession Marjorie, Margie, Mildred, Adele, Mary A, Peggy Lou, Beverley, Shirley, Sherri (twice), Kathy, Paulette, Didi, Bobbie, Demerie, Esther, Gloria, Maria, Lupitia, Eva and then another Mary.'

Announcing that this could be true love at long last, he married Christine, wife number 26, in 1985. 'I feel good about this one,' Mr Wolfe said as he came out of the Last Vegas wedding chapel, where the clerk in charge described the bride as 'a very nice lady except she had a lot of tattoos'.

Addressing reporters after the ceremony, Mr Wolfe said his only reservation about her was that 'she eats sunflower seeds in bed'. It lasted nine months.

He has paid more than one million dollars in alimony and always keeps a couple of wedding dresses handy in the wardrobe. Mr Wolfe has just married a fifteen-year-old called Daisy Delgado.

MOST MIS-SPELT NAME

Edward A. Nedelcov of Regina, Canada smashed all records with an amazing 1,023 mis-spellings of his family name since January 1960. He finds that Nevelcove, Neddlecough, Middlecou and Needochou are quite common versions. However, a letter from the Club Med improved upon these by writing to Edward Nedle and Co. His bank addressed him once as Needleco and later as Nedleson. Even a telegram from a close friend in Sydney accepting a wedding invitation was addressed to B. Heddlegove.

On a receipt for nine extra-large spare ribs from Western Pizzas he was down as Meerinwoz. On a later receipt for nine extra-large chickens he was Petlecode. A third receipt said Nidcole and a fourth, Nuddlecale. At this point he switched to Romano Pizzas who went for Nettlecove.

As a primary school teacher, he has now taken to including his own name in spelling tests. Amidst 'cat', 'bread', and 'please' he inserts 'Mr Nedelcov' with universally wayward results. Kevin Seivewright got it down as Mr Nettlecoke while in her class diary Lisa Mae Clarke wrote: 'Today I started at Mabel Brown School. I am in room number one and my teacher's name is Nevelcod.'

He once wrote to the Queen telling her about his grade seven children. His proudest possession is a reply from Her Majesty addressed to E. A. Dedelcov.

THE LEAST SUCCESSFUL PIGEON RACE

Nothing brings greater excitement to a pigeon race than the complete disappearance of all or most of the competitors. In 1978 6,745 were released at Preston in Lancashire. Of these, 5,545 were never seen again amidst rumours that they had retired to the Devonshire coast.

This record, however, was comprehensively shattered in 1983 when the Northern Ireland Pigeon Racing Society lost 16,430 in one go. Although a handful of duller birds flew straight home in record time, swarms of more adventurous little creatures were later found basking in country gardens all over West Wales. Housewives were asked to leave out rice, lentils and dried peas to build their strength up but, eventually, special transport was laid on for the journey home.

THE MOST OVERDUE LIBRARY BOOK

One of our British borrowers has snatched this world record back from America. Till now the most overdue book in the history of the library services was Dr J. Currie's *Febrile Diseases*, which was taken out of the University of Cincinnati Medical Library in 1823 by Mr M. Dodd and returned by his grandson 135 years later.

But this feat has just been shot to ribbons by a Bishop of Winchester. In 1650 he borrowed the aptly named *Book of Fines* from Somerset county records office. A register of property transactions in Taunton between 1641 and 1648, this volume so enthralled the bishop that it remained in his office for 200 years. It then passed to the Church Commissioners who hung on to it for another century or so.

In 1985 the book was returned to the Somerset county library, having acrued a fine of approximately £3,000.

FASTEST KNOCKOUT

Ralph Walton's fine record of being knocked out in ten and a half seconds lasted only a year and six days so intense is the competition. On 4 November 1947, Pat Brownson saw stars after the first and only punch of his contest against Mike Collins.

This rather special boxer actively contributed to only four seconds of the Golden Gloves Tournament in Minneapolis, Minnesota. He was so far beyond encouragement that they dispensed with the traditional count of ten.

THE MOST REJECTED BOOK MANUSCRIPT

When we last heard of him, Mr Gilbert Young's book, *World Government Crusade*, had been rejected by more publishers than any other manuscript, having been returned 105 times. 'A copy seems to come back every day,' he said in 1973, shortly before writing to the Soviet Ambassador asking if a Russian publisher might be interested.

They were not; and nor were a further 99 British publishers. This brings his total to an almost unbeatable 205 rejection slips, all of which he keeps as souvenirs.

'I am running out of publishers to try,' observed Mr Young, a retired insurance official, whose book outlines the policies of the 'World Government and Old Age Pensioners' Party' that he founded in 1958. His main scheme is to establish one government for the whole world with one police force and one compulsory language. Another of his ideas is to turn Buckingham Palace into an old folks' home.

THE MOST MISPRINTS IN A NEWSPAPER

The Times goes from strength to strength. On 15 March 1978 it achieved an impressive 78 misprints in one page. Among the news items covered were 'Sir Harold Wilson's action in making public an oss.'

Further extending the freedom of the press some three months later, they carried an astonishing 97 errors in only five and a half inches of one story. It concerned Pope Paul VI, who was referred to throughout as 'the Pop', and dwelt upon his 'swping rorganization' of the papal curia.

It said that 'Th Scrtariat of Stat, the vatican's forignoffic, gratly expand, its activitis as Pop Paul pushed normalization of church relations with communist and other countris'. Furthermore, 'Incrased collegiality in th running of th church ld to cration of the synod of Bishops, a large gathering of ky bishops vtry thre yars and an organization to maintain these contacts in between synods.'

In an age when many feel that modern popes have become a shade too populist, this fascinating report does much to restore to the papacy some of its lost mystery.

THE LEAST POPULAR CHRISTIAN NAMES

For many years Mr J. W. Leaver wrote annually to *The Times* with a list of the twenty christian names which had proved most popular around the font during the previous twelve months. The first *Book of Heroic Failures* pointed out with some sadness that he had nowhere listed the twenty least popular. Filling this gap, it dwelt upon the lost beauty of Tram, Brained, Babberley, Despair and Dozer.

The county of Kent, however, has led a heartening revival. In the 1980s a couple there chose to name their child 'Depressed Cupboard Cheesecake', while in the nineteenth century a Richard Garrett christened his son 'Balls' (1810–80). So satisfactory was it that he passed the name on to his second son, who was known as 'Balls Junior'. They lived in Maidstone.

THE FASTEST DEFEAT IN CHESS

Gibaud has been overthrown. Ever since 1924 this French chess master has been revered for achieving defeat in only four moves. A Monsieur Labard played the walk-on part in this great scene.

But in the 1959 US Open Championship somebody called Masefield was a useful foil, moving around the white pieces in a match that enabled the immortal Trinka to be checkmated in three moves:

NEW WORLD RECORDS

P – K4	P – KKt4
Kt – QB3	P – KB4
Q – R5	Mate

THE MOST BORING LECTURE

The previous record holder was Dr David Coward. In 1977 he won the 'Most Boring Lecturer of the Year' contest at Leeds University with an exquisitely dull talk on 'the problems of the manned urinal'. In March 1986, however, he was outclassed by Dr Frank Oliver of Exeter University who delivered an unbeatable lecture on 'Co-efficency correlations'.

With his back to the audience throughout, he explained in a series of comprehensively detailed blackboard diagrams exactly how to 'measure the strength of the relationship between two variables at points between minus one and plus one'. It is a subject which, Dr Oliver says, is 'essentially fascinating'.

So resounding was his triumph in this annual competition that the event was cancelled the following year. No one on the staff felt confident to pit themselves against the reigning title-holder.

When the event was revived in 1988 Dr Oliver won yet again by the simple device of repeating exactly the same lecture.

THE LEAST SUCCESSFUL GARAGE

The previous record holder merely had a garage with four steps up the front. However, in a fearless advance in garage design Mrs Caroline Hitchens decided to incorporate one in the basement of her 'dream home' built on a hillside in Penzance.

Any car parked in this garage would have needed to cross the lawn and several flower beds and then descend a thirty foot cliff to the road. To get out at the back of the house the car would have to burrow up through thirty feet of earth to join the traffic.

THE LEAST SUCCESSFUL DEFROSTING DEVICE

Mr Derek Davies has successfully broken the world record for de-frosting a car door.

While employed in 1960 as third secretary (commercial) at the British Embassy in Vienna, he attended a fancy dress party as Hamlet. His costume featured a borrowed satin blouse, a pair of brightly coloured tights and a wig, while Yorick was represented by a Burmese tiger's skull into the cranium of which was set an ash-tray and a receptacle for matches.

The party went with a swing and Mr Davies's attire was much acclaimed. Snow fell and, when he left, his Morris Minor was com-pletely entombed. The Yorick skull had run out of matches and so he tried to unfreeze the lock with his breath. During this endeavour he became frozen to it and could only wave his Burmese tiger's skull to attract passers-by. He was found by two earnest Viennese policemen who hardly knew which aspect of the case to be alarmed by most.

THE LEAST SUCCESSFUL HUMAN CANNONBALL

In 1972 Miss Mary Connor made three fearless attempts to become the first woman ever to be blasted across the River Avon.

On the first occasion the cannon fired and nothing happened. On the second the cannon went off at half cock and she swept gracefully into the air getting at least half-way across the river.

However, her personal best came on the third attempt when she arrived, wearing a bandage round her ankle and plasters on both elbows, while explaining to bystanders that she had grazed them coming out of the cannon. She not only flew out this time and went into the river, back first, at exactly the same spot, but also capsized the rescue boat and had to swim to the bank.

This entirely surpasses the previous record, held by Miss Rita

Thunderbird, who remained in the cannon while her bra was shot across the River Thames.

NEW ADVANCES IN AMERICAN FOOTBALL

The greatest-ever exponent of American football was Jim Marshall of the Minnesota Vikings. On 26 October 1964 in a match against the San Francisco 49ers he crowned a glorious career by snatching a 49er fumble, sprinting sixty yards the wrong way down Kezar Stadium and scoring for the opposition. This sort of touchdown is much harder to achieve because you have to beat the defensive attempts of not only the opposing side, but also your own team.

No one could believe this marvellous display of skill and in no time the entire Minnesota bench was chasing down the sideline, waving their arms at him violently. With his mind very much on the job, Marshall said that he 'didn't hear anybody yelling', but construed his colleagues' behaviour as understandable excitement.

With a modesty common to all great athletes he said: 'I just picked the ball up and started running. I guess I just got turned around.'

TWO

1980 – A VINTAGE YEAR

In which power goes to a robot's head; an American fisherman thinks the world is coming to an end; and the cream of British womanhood explores new ways to negotiate a roundabout.

WORST PRODUCTION OF *MACBETH*

In September 1980 crowds poured into the Old Vic Theatre in London to see Peter O'Toole's unforgettable *Macbeth*, which is widely held to have basked in the worst set of theatrical notices in modern times.

Eradicating the unnecessarily tragic aspects that have always weighed the play down, the cast sent the first-night audience home rocking with happy laughter. One critic after another rose up to acknowledge the astonishing qualities of this production.

The greatest acclaim was reserved for the unexpected qualities of Mr O'Toole's performance.

The *Daily Mail* observed that 'it was, of course, the rottenest luck for him to run smack into a wall on his third bravura exit (so much of the play takes place in the dark)'.

Another critic noticed that the three glamorous witches were not 'foul, unnatural hags', as Shakespeare absurdly suggests. Dressed in white chiffon gowns, they 'look as if they shop at Fortnum and Masons'.

The *London Evening News* drew attention to the new-age Lady Macbeth who 'greeted her husband by leaping at him and achieving a leg-encircling embrace of the kind which illustrates helpful sex manuals'. Her generally dramatic style, he said, 'would have woken the whole castle'.

In no time coach parties began arriving at the Old Vic where the run was soon sold out. From the London and provincial runs it earned a quarter of a million pounds, making it one of the most profitable *Macbeth*s on record. 'I was born to play this part,' Mr O'Toole said later.

THE LEAST SUCCESSFUL OIL DRILLERS

Erecting the very latest equipment, Texaco workmen set about drilling for oil at Lake Peigneur in Louisiana during November 1980.

After only a few hours drilling they sat back expecting oil to shoot up. Instead, however, they watched a whirlpool form, sucking down not only the entire 1,300-acre lake, but also five houses, nine barges, eight tug boats, two oil-rigs, a mobile home, most of a botanical garden and ten per cent of nearby Jefferson Island, leaving a half-mile-wide crater. No one told them there was an abandoned salt mine underneath.

A local fisherman said he thought the world was coming to an end.

THE LEAST SUCCESSFUL DEMOLITION

In December 1980 Solihull Council hired a local firm of contractors to demolish a row of delapidated cowsheds on the Stratford Road near Birmingham.

Early on Sunday morning eyewitnesses saw an excavator moving at speed along the road. When it came to the cowsheds, it turned off on the wrong side and headed without pause for Monkspath Hall, a listed eighteenth century building set in fields with a tree-lined approach and rated as one of the most famous farmhouses in the Midlands.

In forty-five minutes the building was reduced to a heap of rubble.

THE LEAST SUCCESSFUL ATTEMPT TO MURDER A SPOUSE

Dwarfing all known records for matrimonial homicide, Mr Peter Scott of Southsea made seven attempts to kill his wife without her once noticing that anything was wrong.

In 1980 he took out an insurance policy on his good lady which would bring him £250,000 in the event of her accidental death. Soon afterwards he placed a lethal dose of mercury in her strawberry flan, but it all rolled out. Not wishing to waste this deadly substance, he next stuffed her mackerel with the entire contents of the bottle. This time she ate it, but with no side-effects whatsoever.

Warming to the task, he then took his better half on holiday to Yugoslavia. Recommending the panoramic views, he invited her to sit on the edge of a cliff. She declined to do so, prompted by what she later described as some 'sixth sense'. The same occurred only weeks later when he urged her to savour the view from Beachy Head.

While his spouse was in bed with chicken-pox he started a fire outside her bedroom door, but some interfering busybody put it out. Undeterred, he started another fire and burnt down the entire flat at Taswell Road, Southsea. The wife of his bosom escaped uninjured.

Another time he asked her to stand in the middle of the road so that he could drive towards her and check if his brakes were working.

At no time did Mrs Scott feel that the magic had gone out of their marriage. Since it appeared nothing short of a small nuclear bomb would have alerted this good woman to her husband's intentions, he eventually gave up and confessed everything to the police. After the case a detective said that Mrs Scott had been 'absolutely shattered' when told of her husband's plot to kill her. 'She had not twigged it at all and was dumbstruck.'

THE LEAST SUCCESSFUL AGONY AUNT

This honour falls to the outstanding Rose Shepherd who wrote the agony column on *Honey* magazine in 1980. From the day of her appointment onwards she did not receive a single reader's letter. When, months later, a few actually did arrive, this fine woman announced that she could not solve any of them.

'They asked impossible questions like "I eat cigarette tobacco. Is this wrong?" It was hopeless.' Deciding that people's problems are basically insoluble, she resigned.

THE LEAST SUCCESSFUL FUN FESTIVAL

In October 1980 Chichester hosted a fun festival that promised 'a weekend that was different'. The organizers kept their word.

The British all-comers dog swimming race was called off when not a single owner entered his pet; the pie-eating contest was won by a man who consumed just three and a half pies; the helicopter rides were cancelled because of bad weather; the parachute display was called off because the landing-site was too close to the A27; the Elvis Presley lookalike, 'Rupert', was delayed by a road accident, and when he eventually arrived there were so few spectators the act was shelved.

When by 3 o'clock nothing had happened at all, a lively crowd formed around the organizers' tent. Inexplicably, they were not enjoying this feast of entertainment. Loud among the voices of complaint was Mr R. Farncombe who had come all the way from West Worthing:

'I went mostly to see Rupert who was not there, for a helicopter ride we never got and wrestling which did not exist. Thank goodness we didn't arrive till 12.30.' He was offered free tickets for the next day when the high spot was a hot-air balloon which failed to turn up.

THE LEAST SATISFACTORY ROBOT

Seeking greater efficiency, the Kavio Restaurant in Leith bought Donic, a robot programmed as a wine waiter. In the summer of 1980 they dressed it in a black hat and bow tie, fitted the batteries and turned on.

Showing a natural flair for the work, this advanced machine ran amok, smashed the furniture, poured wine all over the carpet and frightened the diners until its lights went out, its voice box packed up and its head dropped off in a customer's lap. When asked to account for this outstanding performance, the robot's manufacturer said that he had given the operating instructions to the restaurant's disc-jockey.

THE LEAST SUCCESSFUL WEDDING RECEPTION

Newly-weds John and Barbara Besio claimed this record at the Blue Dolphin restaurant in Los Angeles during 1980.

The reception made a promising start when the groom's father expressed the wish to dance upon the table. So unbridled was this performance that the manager called the police. In the resulting fracas five policemen were injured and six wedding guests arrested.

At this point the bride asked what kind of family she was marrying into, whereupon the groom departed from the usual custom, picked up the entire wedding-cake and pushed it in her face. When fighting broke out between the happy couple, the police were called again and threatened to arrest them. Guests waving off the newly-weds in the going-away car noticed that Mrs Besio, as we must now call her, landed a blow which appeared to temporarily stun her husband, bringing peace to an otherwise perfect occasion.

THE LEAST SUCCESSFUL WEDDING TOAST

Like all proud fathers, Grigory Romanov, the mayor of Leningrad, wanted the very best for his daughter's wedding. In January 1980 this senior member of the Soviet Politburo persuaded the director of the city's Hermitage Museum to lend him Catherine the Great's china tea-set especially for the occasion.

Late in the exuberant proceedings one guest got to his feet and accidentally dropped a cup. Thinking that this was a toast, the other guests took it as a signal for the traditional gesture of good luck, whereupon they all rose to their feet and hurled the entire service into the fireplace.

THE MOST POINTLESS BANK RAID

With split-second timing and consummate teamwork four masked men raided a bank at Artema near Rome in February 1980. Not knowing that the bank had closed three minutes early 'because things were quiet', the gang's leader ran headlong into a locked plate-glass door and knocked himself out.

Falling back into the arms of three accomplices, he was carried to the waiting getaway car and driven off. According to bank officials, this complex raid was completed in just under four minutes.

THE LEAST SUCCESSFUL LEARNER DRIVER

Now that Mrs Miriam Hargreaves, the world record holder, has let us all down by passing her driving test at the fortieth attempt the field becomes wide open for a promising newcomer. Many doubters felt, however, that her dazzling total of 212 lessons would be un-surpassed. Oh ye of little faith . . .

By March 1980 the sprightly Mrs Betty Tudor of Exeter had been learning for nineteen years and clocked up a breath-taking 273 lessons. In this time she had nine instructors and was banned from three driving schools. She only put in for seven tests and failed them all with flying colours.

Her seventh ended when she drove the wrong way round a roundabout, whereupon the examiner screamed at her and said that he would drive from then on. Mrs Tudor told him that 'if it hadn't been for the cars ˙coming in the opposite direction, hooting, he wouldn't have noticed anything wrong'.

Although Mrs Tudor has now decided to sell the car, one suspects that she is only resting. You cannot keep a talent of that magnitude down for long.

THE PLAN THAT FAILED

The plan: One night in May 1980 David Barber would enter Cheltenham Co-op with a bag full of equipment to break into a steel and reinforced-concrete safe. After removing countless thousands he would hide them, with his equipment, in his bag and make his escape disguised in a jogging suit bought specially for the occasion.

What actually happened: He broke into the Co-op and was drilling away from the moment he arrived until shortly before dawn. He was just going through the last metal barrier when the door swung open of its own accord, having been unlocked throughout. The safe turned out to be empty. When he made his getaway next morning his bag was found in its hiding place by schoolboys who took it to the police. It was bugged ready for his return.

THE SOLDIER WHO CAUSED MOST CHAOS

In the military world Dan Raschen has few peers. While still in his twenties, his career had been sufficiently varied and spectacular to provide the material for an entire volume of autobiography entitled, *Wrong Again, Dan!* The following can only hint at his distinguished range of achievements:

On the way to India in 1944 to join his regiment he lost all his underwear and his only pair of pyjamas while washing them out of a porthole. All the ship's cutlery went the same way when he threw out a basin of dishwater. The troops had to eat with their fingers for the rest of the voyage.

On arrival he was instantly accused of murder. The case only foundered when he pointed at his supposed victim grinning cheerfully in a growing crowd of onlookers.

So enthusiastic was his performance during tests for a commission that after the obstacle course he had to wait for other less interesting candidates to finish so they could come back and rescue him from beneath a railway sleeper.

While in charge of three amphibious weasel tanks, he lost all of them in one week. Two got stuck in a pond and one went through the wall of his own accommodation.

For one so exquisitely disaster-prone, a career in explosives was the inevitable course. After an intense period of training he arrived at the South Pacific to blow up some coral reef, never having attempted it before. His finest hour came when he moored his own boat to the very bit of reef that was receiving his closest attention.

'One likes to think there are people who have been worse, but admittedly it does seem unlikely,' says the great man. Those wishing to study his exploits in more detail should apply for his memoirs to Buckland Press at 125 High Holborn, London WC1.

THREE

THE BRITISH WAY
OF DOING THINGS

In which pigs, greyhounds and chess mas-
ters fly the flag; gardeners are forced to
read about Avonearly beetroot; and Mr
Brown's postcard arrives.

THE LEAST SUCCESSFUL CLUB

The Langworth Pig Club was set up to give owners insurance for their pigs, tips on pig health and general talks on all matters relating to the advancement of the pig in general.

This fine club reached its peak in January 1988 when all the members admitted that none of them owned a pig. Most had not done so for fifteen years and some had not even seen one during this period. This heartening state of affairs was ruined by Mr George Abbott, who combined the visiting of sick pigs and pig ear-piercing with being the local Methodist minister. He closed the club down on the grounds that no one had attended the AGM at his house in Barlins Road for the second year running.

THE LEAST ACCURATE INDEX

So often indexes are nothing more than dull signposts to a book's contents. In 1981 however, the index in the *Gardener's World Vegetable Book* transcended mere utilitarianism and was hailed as a work of art in its own right, because it bore no resemblance to the book's contents whatsoever.

Page 25, for example, is not devoted to Avoncrisp lettuce at all, but to helpful hints on planting tubers with a trowel. Furthermore, page 52 is not remotely connected with chickweed, being obsessed with the altogether more absorbing topic of cures for cabbage root fly.

The index is particularly fond of page 16 and sends readers there on no less than fifteen occasions, seeking aubergines, broad beans, two strains of beetroot (Avonearly and Boltardy), cloches, courgettes, cucumber, deep bed method, lettuce, uses of the Melbourne frame, marrow, melon, early peas, peppers, sweet corn and bush tomatoes. It is, in fact, solely concerned with the humble cabbage.

Of the 177 entries listed a magnificent 166 give bold directions to the wrong pages.

THE LEAST SUCCESSFUL TOURIST RESORT

Tired of its reputation as Britain's least attractive town, the inhabitants of Slough decided to relaunch the place as a tourist resort. In October 1987 they bombarded the nation with advertising for 'a dream weekend in Slough' that asked: 'Why bother with Paris, Venice or Mustique when you can spend a once-in-a-lifetime weekend in Slough, the Cannes of the north and the Hollywood of Berkshire for only £75?'

'Pig out on the world's best junk food,' said the leaflets, offering a unique package break at the Holiday Inn with a weekly season ticket to the local Maybox cinema.

The price included a tour of Slough Trading Estate, Slough Community Centre ('once famous as the home base of the Ada Umsworth Old Formation Dance Team') and the car park next to the Mars Bar factory, 'which was used as the location for a dramatic scene in a seven-minute sci-fi film made in 1986 by a student at the National Film School'.

Not a single inquiry was received.

THE LEAST CORRECT ASTROLOGER

The jewel in Fleet Street's crown during the 1930s and 1940s was the astrology column of R. H. Naylor in the *Sunday Express*. In the space of a few weeks this outstanding man predicted that Franco would never rule Spain, that a united Ireland was imminent and that 'war is not scheduled for 1939'. He explained that 'Hitler's horoscope shows he is not a war maker', while admitting that Germany 'might at some point show interest in regaining Togoland'.

On the domestic front he predicted a general election on 7 November 1938, at which the new government would gain a slender majority. The next election did not take place until 1945 and it was a landslide victory for the Labour Party.

With his unique insights into the future Naylor foresaw that 'Bolshevism and Nazism would co-operate' and said so days before Germany invaded Russia. He also predicted that 'aircraft which cannot hover will soon be deemed utterly useless' and that 'Iceland will become a key area'.

THE NOT TERRIBLY GOOD SAMARITAN

Being a kind-hearted sort of chap, Mr Hugh Pike rushed to the aid of a British family in distress in 1978.

They were on holiday in Bordeaux. Their Morris Estate car had broken down. They needed a spare part from Britain so they had to abandon the vehicle. They spoke no French. They couldn't get back to Boulogne for the boat home. It was now Sunday night and the father had to be at work in his native Sheffield by 8 a.m. the next morning. The situation was almost perfect.

Wishing to help, Mr Pike told them he had a working knowledge of French, was himself going to Paris and would be only too pleased to assist. He raced them at high speed to the Gare du Nord, arrived with seconds to spare, went to the ticket desk, asked a guard for the train to Boulogne, dashed down platform six, and got the Sheffield family on board, as the train pulled out amidst dewy-eyed protestations of undying gratitude and friendship.

Only as he walked back down the platform, aglow with the knowledge of a good deed done, did he look up at the noticeboard and realize that he had put them on a train to Bologna in Italy, a country with whose ways and languages they were even less well acquainted.

THE LEAST SUCCESSFUL MEN'S RIGHTS GROUP

Inspired by the success of the American Coalition of Free Men (it has 800 affiliated groups and regular meetings to campaign for men's rights), Mr Arthur Murray decided in 1983 to set up a UK branch. Since then it has attracted no members whatsoever. The regular newsletter consists of Arthur pleading with his six best friends to join.

When a reporter from *The Times* went to investigate 'the group', he found that Arthur was under constant attack from his wife, a veteran feminist who is bigger than he is, owns the house, supports Arthur financially and makes him do all the housework.

THE WORST SUBMARINE

The conventional submarine, rising and descending at will, is of only limited interest to our sort of student. It does not compare with the more versatile K-boats which the British developed in 1917.

K-1 sank after colliding with K-4 off the Danish coast. K-2 caught fire on its first test dive. K-3 plunged inexplicably to the sea bed with the Prince of Wales on board, eventually re-surfacing only to sink after being rammed by K-6. K-4 ran aground, K-5 foundered in the Bay of Biscay.

K-14 sprang a leak before its first trial and during one celebrated manoeuvre in the North Sea it collided with K-22, which used to be K-13 but was renamed after it keeled over at Loch Gare in Scotland while on seaworthiness trials. K-14 sank, while K-22 was damaged beyond repair after getting in the way of HMS *Inflexible*, a cruiser which happened to be passing.

In the same manoeuvre K-17 was struck by HMS *Fearless*, having already been hit by K-7, thereby incapacitating itself. On observing this mayhem, K-4 stopped engines, altered course and was rammed by K-6 which later got stuck on the ocean bed. Better still, K-15 sank in Portsmouth Harbour before going anywhere or doing anything.

Ks 18, 19, 20 and 21 were never completed, but their keels were modified for use in the new M range. M-1 was rammed by a merchant vessel while on diving patrol in the channel and M-2 sank after springing a leak.

THE LEAST SUCCESSFUL RESEARCH

While writing the history of his village, the vicar of Eye, near Peterborough, decided to include thumbnail sketches of 'pillars of society' over the centuries.

The Reverend Phillip Randall was particularly impressed by a tombstone inside St Matthew's church, which bore the initials 'H.W.P.' Because of its prominent position, he wisely concluded that this must be the grave of some extremely important local dignitary.

He was so fascinated by it that he pored over parish records for nine years in hope of finding a Henry Wimbourne Potter or a Herbert Wattle Pitstock or a Happy Washwater O'Pudding.

Almost a decade of research yielded not one person with these initials. The vicar was, however, able to hazard an informed guess that the tombstone was eighteenth-century because of the florid style of its inscription.

Eventually, in 1971 he gave up and put a final appeal for information in the parish magazine. Two days later a parishioner telephoned to say that his father helped lay the stone to mark the Hot Water Pipe.

THE WORLD'S WORST BOOKBINDER

The highspot of the London Book Fair was a fabulous craft exhibition entitled 'Hideous Bindings'. It featured the whole spectrum of book covers, ranging from those that would not open at all to those that opened with a crack and and then would not shut. The winner was a most sympathetic modern design that combined all these features.

The exhibits were all entries for the B. F. Hardwick Award, which is given annually to those book covers, ancient or modern, which display the most brutal disregard for their contents. A classic in this genre is a biography of Pope Pius XII which has a 45-RPM record glued to the cover with the back of the supreme pontiff's head on the label. Much admired was *God's Revenge Against Murder*, which was rebound in 1977 with soiled bandages by a gentleman from Bristol.

Widely acknowledged as the world's worst bookbinder, Hardwick himself produced instantly recognizable work. His trade marks were heavily tanned pigskin covers that reduce to powder with handling and a tendency to trim page margins so neatly that the text is helpfully diminished.

THE LEAST ACCURATE TOURIST GUIDE

Holidaymakers drove round and round in circles, exploring the West of England fully, thanks to a new map given away free by Godfrey Davis Rentacar and Best Western Hotels in 1983.

It marked Taunton as a surfing centre, even though it is fifteen miles from the sea. Furthermore, it placed a racecourse in the heart of the small Devonshire village of Chudleigh and marked Axminster down as having a grand prix circuit. Underwater activities were symbolized by a racing car and windmills by a pick and shovel.

A Godfrey Davis executive said: 'At least we got the roads right.'

THE LEAST COMPREHENSIBLE LEGISLATION

An exciting new contender for this title is the law defining how dentists should work out their salaries:

The following paragraph shall be substituted for paragraph (ii) of regulation three of the amended regulations:
(ii) In any succeeding month in the same year the remuneration

shall not exceed such sum as will, when added to the remuneration of the previous months of the year, amount to the product of the standard sum multiplied by the number of months of the year which will have expired at the end of the month in respect of which the calculation is being made together with one half of any authorized fees in excess of that product which but for the provisions of this regulation would have been payable in those months, excluding for all the purposes of this paragraph the month of January 1949.

It is still not, however, quite equal to the classic regulation concerning ground nuts:

'In the Nuts (unground), (other than ground nuts) Order, the expression nuts shall have reference to such nuts, other than ground nuts, as would but for this amending Order not qualify as nuts (unground) (other than ground nuts) by reason of their being nuts (unground).'

THE SLOWEST POSTAL DELIVERY

So infuriated was Mr J. F. Brown of Hampstead, London, by the sex manuals which had appeared on his local library's shelves that he sat down straight away and wrote a letter of complaint, dated 14 July 1938.

Trembling with indignation, he immediately posted his irate missive, which suggested that 'all these disgusting books by Havelock Ellis and similarly dirty-minded men posing as psychiatrists be removed from your shelves. Nay sir, I do more than suggest it, I demand it. You are contributing to the undermining of the fibre of the English people. And if war comes, as it most certainly will, we shall be in no state to wage it'.

Although the library was only a mile away from his home address, his letter arrived in 1976, thirty-eight years, seven months, five weeks and one day later, by which time the librarian had died and the library had been closed in a merger with Camden.

HOW TO VISIT LOVED ONES

The art of visiting relatives was significantly enhanced by Dr John Fellows of Dorset in March 1984. Having bought a £600 return air ticket to New York, he flew to John F. Kennedy Airport. On arrival, however, he found that he could not remember his daughter's address.

Most of us could have managed this, but Dr Fellows went one further and found that he was also unable to remember her name. Thus equipped, he spent several hours at the airport trying to recall it before catching the next plane home. 'I was tired,' he explained.

THE LEAST TOP SECRET BASE

RAF Caerwent was a NATO base shrouded in the utmost mystery. What was it for? What was in there? Why was it so secret?

No one knew – until a rambler's map for the district was produced showing every last detail of the base with an exact scale drawing of its layout, including the highly sensitive arms depot.

The map was produced by the Forestry Commission in 1976 after a series of aerial photographs. When the Ministry of Defence found out and banned it five years later, 2,000 copies had already been sold to enthusiastic ramblers and holidaymakers.

OUR OWN CHESS MASTER

To his utter amazement Mr Geoffrey Hosking, an Englishman studying at Moscow University, was invited to take part in the 1965 Baku International Chess Tournament.

It transpired that they were short of foreign players and a Russian friend had put his name forward on the strength of Hosking's vodka-fuelled victory in a casual friendly game that neither of them could remember with any clarity.

Hosking not only lost all twelve games in Baku, but also played them in such a way that the Tournament Bulletin refused to publish the customary match details on the grounds that they were not up to scratch.

THE LEAST SUCCESSFUL GREYHOUND

This outstanding animal, called 'Mental's Last Hope', took part in the 8.15 race at Wimbledon on 29 March 1961. Not only did it come in last, but it was so ecstatic with the result that it refused to stop running.

After fifteen minutes they decided to release the hare again in the hope of distracting the dog, but to no avail. The creature was too overjoyed to be affected by a mechanical object.

Track officials were called in to help and in no time this enthusiastic animal was leading a field of fifty people in hot pursuit. For thirty minutes and twenty-nine seconds the crowd was treated to one of the most memorable races in the history of this sport. 'We had to wait until it got exhausted and gave itself up,' an official said.

THE LEAST SUCCESSFUL DAY TRIP

Few people have packed more into a day trip than Michael and Lilian Long from Kent who went to Boulogne in May 1987. On Easter Sunday this adventurous couple went for a short walk around the town. In no time they were spectacularly lost and showing all the qualities of born explorers.

'We walked and walked,' Mrs Long recalled, 'and the further we

walked to try to get back, the further we walked away from Boulogne.'

They walked throughout the night and finally hitched a lift next morning to a small village they did not recognize. Here they caught a train to Paris. In the pleasure-loving French capital they spent all their remaining money on catching what they thought was the train to Boulogne. After an enjoyable trip they arrived in Luxembourg at midnight on Monday.

Two hours later police put them on the train back to Paris, but it divided and their half ended up in Basle, an attractive medieval town in the north of Switzerland.

Having no money, they tried to find work, but without success. The rail authorities offered them a free warrant back to Belfort, thinking this was where they had come from, whereupon this intrepid pair walked forty-two miles to Vesoul, hitched a lift to Paris and nearly boarded the train to Bonn in Germany.

Diverted to the right platform, they reached Boulogne a week after they had set out on their walk. When he arrived at Dover, Mr Long said this was their first trip abroad and they would not be leaving England again.

WORST TRANSATLANTIC YACHTSMAN

Crossing the Atlantic single-handed is a challenge attempted by only the greatest yatchsmen and women. The most important of these for us is the immortal Mr Sebury who made two historic attempts.

On 31 August 1986, he set sail from Newport, Gwent, in a fifteen-foot sloop specially equipped with a bucket full of cheese, five litres of orange juice and an ordnance survey map of the Welsh coast. Three days later he found himself adrift with his mast down and engine broken. He got just beyond the Bristol Channel, where he became a martyr to seasickness and moored the boat in the middle of a Royal Naval Torpedo range. When an official craft went out to warn him, they found Mr Sebury slumped on the side of his vessel shouting: 'Take me ashore and sink the boat.'

Encouraged by this, he made a second attempt to cross the Atlantic later that year and got as far as Milford Haven.

THE MOST CHAOTIC WEDDING SERVICE

New life was breathed into the dull nuptial routine at Eltham Parish Church during May 1972.

The vicar was only two words into the service ('Dearly beloved') when he downed tools because the bride's brother was panning his whirring cine-camera across the congregation and lingering on the choirgirls with his zoom lens.

A shouting match broke out between the two men and 120 guests saw the bride's father stand up to ask why if the Queen could have a cameraman in the church, his daughter couldn't?

At the signing of the register there was jostling and shouting in the vestry. And, as the couple walked down the aisle, the organist was just launching into the theme tune from *Dr Zhivago* at the bride's request when there appeared in the doorway what the vicar later described as 'a scraggy-looking bagpiper' playing 'Amazing Grace'.

Mr George Tubbs, the verger, valiantly tried to bar his way, whereupon the bride's father challenged the vicar to a boxing match.

Mr Tubbs, who is seventy-two, said: 'I've done over a hundred weddings in the past two years but this one beats the lot.'

THE WORST HOUSEHOLD ORNAMENT

For thirty years Mrs Doreen Burley polished her favourite ornament every day. She allowed her five grandchildren to play with it and usually gave the brass orb pride of place on the mantelpiece at her home in Rawtenstall, Lancashire.

Only in March 1988 did she discover it was a live bomb. When she described her pride and joy to the manager of an antique shop, he advised her to call the police.

The army arrived next day and carried it off as though it was priceless china. 'I just couldn't believe I had been polishing a bomb all this time,' Mrs Burley said. 'I must have picked it up in a box of brasses in Bradford.'

FOUR

ENCOURAGING NEWS FROM THE UNITED STATES OF AMERICA

In which a cannibal goes into the cafeteria;
Abraham Lincoln gets his rocks off; and
Mrs Garcia dresses up as a Red Indian.

LEAST INTERESTING LIVE TV SHOW

In April 1986 the WGN TV station got a scoop. Amidst much ballyhoo they announced they were going to unseal Al Capone's secret vault beneath the Lexington Hotel, Chicago. It was said to contain hoards of missing money, diamonds, whisky and the bones of those who had 'upset' him.

Entitled, 'The Mystery of Al Capone's Vaults', the two-hour live show was hosted by an excited reporter who wore an excavation helmet and a large fighter pilot's moustache. 'I am Geraldo Rivera and you're about to witness a live television event,' he gasped. 'Now for the first time that vault is going to be opened live. This is an adventure you and I will take together.'

The show was syndicated across the whole of America and there was a carnival-like atmosphere with hundreds celebrating at an 'Al Capone Safe-Cracking Charity Ball'. Also in attendance was a small army of law enforcement officials, reporters, Internal Revenue agents, members of the federal treasury, claiming that Capone still owed them $800,000 and criminal technicians who were there gathering evidence.

To add an air of authenticy to the production, Rivera demonstrated the use of a prohibition-era Thompson sub-machine gun and detonated a dynamite blast using a Capone-style plunger.

Tension mounted as an explosives team arrived. After an hour and a half blasting through walls the dust settled and the cameras went in accompanied by Dr Robert Stein, the County Medical Examiner, who was on hand in case bones or mummified bodies were found.

The vault contained two empty gin bottles and Geraldo filled in the time by singing 'Chicago'.

ORATORY AT ITS PEAK

In 1841 General William Henry Harrison was elected president of the United States of America. To mark the occasion he wrote an inaugural speech that was so long and turgid his own party banned him from delivering it.

This rousing address was largely compiled from schoolboy memories of Plutarch and the general was extremely proud of it. Nonetheless, the Republicans got in Daniel Webster, the lexicographer, to rewrite it.

After a whole day's work on the speech Webster was so white, haggard and late for a dinner party that his alarmed hostess said, 'Daniel, I hope nothing has happened.' Webster replied that he had just 'killed seventeen Roman proconsuls as dead as smelts'.

Even in its severely edited form, the speech still lasted an hour and forty minutes and took up ninety-one and a half inches of microscopic print in the *New York Evening Post*. On the coldest day of the year the general delivered his inaugural address, without the protection of a hat or coat, during which he caught pneumionia, died and never held office.

THE LEAST SUCCESSFUL MEMORIAL

The building of a new staff canteen in 1977 gave the US Department of Agriculture the opportunity to commemorate a famous nineteenth-century Colorado pioneer.

Amidst a blaze of enthusiastic publicity the Agriculture Secretary, Robert Bergland, opened 'The Alfred Packer Memorial Dining Facility', with the words: 'Alfred Packer exemplifies the spirit and fare that this agriculture department cafeteria will provide.'

Several months later the cafeteria was renamed when it was discovered that Packer had been convicted of murdering and eating five prospectors in 1874.

THE LEAST SUCCESSFUL BUFFALO CHIP
THROWING CONTEST

The National Buffalo Chip Throwing Contest of 1979 at Athol in Maryland got off to a cracking start when organizers failed to appreciate that there were no buffaloes for 500 miles, that no chips were available except on emergency order by air-freight and that the airline at Laramie, Wyoming, had refused to carry them on grounds of hygiene.

Cow pats were officially ruled a suitable substitute, at which point Dr Philip Ball of Muncie, Indiana, arrived with bursitis in his throwing shoulder. During his first lob he developed 'sudden malfunction of gyro control', whereupon the chip turned through a 90-degree angle and knocked out the event judge. His second lob shattered in mid-air showering much of the audience, who began to go home.

Dr Ball sustained this level of performance throughout. He not only came twenty-third out of twenty-three, but also won the award for Mr Congeniality and for the cow chip thrower with the best mental attitude.

*Footnote for non-American students – It is the practice of cow pokes with free time in the USA to hurl 100 per cent organic buffalo faeces in a competitive spirit. Distances of anything up to 250 feet can be attained.

THE HEAVIEST DEFEAT IN AMERICAN FOOTBALL

Sylvia High School shot into the record books in November 1927 when they played a crucial part in their 270–0 defeat by Haven High. In theory it is impossible to score one touchdown every minute, but Sylvia don't know the meaning of the word.

Sensing the horribly skilful nature of the opposition, they left the pitch and were half-way to the dressing room when their coach,

Frank Brownlee, persuaded them back out. At this point they wisely decided to refrain from tackling anyone or running with the ball should it land anywhere near them.

According to Milliard Kincaid, a Haven player: 'They could have kept the final score down just by taking the ball but they didn't want to do that.'

Of course, not. Instead, they all sat down in the middle of the field and got to know each other.

THE LEAST SUCCESSFUL SAFETY CAMPAIGN

The accolade here goes to the Consumer Product Safety Commission of Washington who in 1974 brought out 80,000 promotional buttons for its Pre-Christmas campaign, bearing the words: 'For Kids' Sake, Think Toy Safety.'

All 80,000 were withdrawn when the commission found that the buttons had sharp edges, parts a child could swallow and paint with a dangerously high lead content.

THE LEAST SUCCESSFUL COMMUNITY CENTRE

The runaway champion in this category is the $280,000 Merrill Township Community Centre in Michigan which opened in 1976 and had no visitors whatsoever. It was eventually discovered three years later, having collapsed under a load of snow, by a solitary woodsman who was out shooting rabbits.

A spokesman for the project said that although it planned a full programme of counselling, barn dances and literacy classes designed to create a new community spirit in remotest Michigan, it was 'built in the middle of a virtually inaccessible forest' and money ran out for the road.

THE LEAST SUCCESSFUL FIRE-PROOFING

The world's first fire-proof theatre, the Iroquois, opened in Chicago on 1 December 1903.

Just thirty days later, as a double octet was launching into a close harmony version of 'In the Pale Moonlight', a faulty blue light bulb used to create a subtle lunar effect set fire to the scenery. The safety curtain jammed two-thirds of the way down, the audience was asked to leave and the theatre burnt to the ground.

MOST LOST MOTORIST

Far too many Sunday drivers are happy to pootle around for a weekend hour or two following dull itineraries. Only Mr Joseph Stophel of Dunedin in Georgia has transformed this activity into the adventure of a lifetime.

Announcing that he was going out for a short drive in September 1987, Mr Stophel took a wrong turning and got happily lost in the dense network of twisting backroads. Three days later he was the subject of a nationwide search with regular bulletins on every radio station.

Seven days later Ms Kathleen Stubblefield passed his car as far away as Indiana. She chased after him and flagged him down. Relaxing at the Stubblefield residence in Blairsville, Mr Stophel said he had travelled 1,700 miles in the past week. It appears that he had motored extensively in several states including Tennessee, Indiana and Kentucky.

THE LEAST SUCCESSFUL MALE CHAUVINIST

Sick of hearing about female equality, Mr Bobby Riggs challenged Billie Jean King to a 'battle of the sexes' tennis match. 'I want to set Women's Lib back twenty years, to get women back in the home where they belong,' he said, adding that they are at their prettiest when they're barefoot, pregnant, taking care of the kiddies and doing the housework.

Although he had not been Wimbledon champion since 1939, he told a press conference before the match on 20 September 1973 that natural male superiority would be enough to defeat the reigning women's champion. 'I will scrape her up,' he said. 'She is a woman and is subject to women's emotional frailties. She will crack up during the match.'

In front of 39,000 people, the largest crowd in tennis history, Mrs King thrashed him 6–4, 6–3, 6–3.

THE LEAST SUCCESSFUL SUICIDE

Tired of life and its assorted awfulness, Ms Elvita Adams decided in 1979 to jump off the 86th floor of the Empire State Building. She said 'goodbye' to the world and leaped, whereupon a sudden gust of wind blew her back into the 85th floor, merely invigorated by the fresh air and exercise.

THE WORST QUIZ SHOW

The worst quiz show ever broadcast on television was 'You're In The Picture', which graced American screens in January 1961. It was taken off by universal acclaim after one instalment.

The programme was hosted by Jackie Gleason, who habitually signs his letters 'The Great Gleason'. It is now possible to see why. In this show, celebrity panellists had to stick their heads through holes in a plyboard screen and ask him questions in order to discover what was painted on the other side.

Due to the fascinating obscurity of these scenes ('The Raising of The Old Glory At Squirri Barri', for example) there was no way that a guest could identify them unless equipped with the most advanced psychic abilities.

On the next week's show Gleason pitched up on his own.

'Ladies and gentlemen', he said, 'I think you'll notice that there is no panel tonight.' Furthermore, there was a 100 per cent absence of painted plyboard scenes. Instead he sat there, drinking a cup of coffee that was 'chock-full-o-booze' while saying what a flop last week's show had been.

After a thirty-minute post-mortem, interlaced with jokes and personal reminiscences, he said: 'I don't know what we're going to do, but tune in next week for the greatest soapless opera you've ever seen.'

Audiences could hardly wait for next week's show when Gleason once again appeared on his own until joined by a chimpanzee. It was not until the third instalment that he risked having another human on the show, by which time Kelloggs had withdrawn sponsorship on the grounds that it was no longer a quiz programme.

THE WORST CELEBRATIONS

Human Kindness Day took place in Washington DC on 10 May 1975. At a press conference afterwards police said there had been 600 arrests, 150 smashed windows, 42 looted refreshment stands, 17 stonings of uniformed officers, 33 fires and 120 cases of public brawling. Furthermore, fourteen cars had been demolished in Constitution Avenue.

Miss Carol Kirkendall, a spokeswoman for the organizers, said that 'although sporadic rock-throwing, public mayhem and purse-snatchings had been a sadness, a lot of beautiful things were going on out there'.

THE LEAST SUCCESSFUL AWARD CEREMONY .

The American Institute of Architects held their 1979 annual conference in Kansas City so as to be near the Kemper Arena, to which they had awarded their prize as 'one of the finest buildings in the nation'.

On the first day of the conference hordes of architects toured this inspired structure with its wide spanning roof trusses, which The Architectural Record described as having 'an almost awesome muscularity'.

On the second day it fell down, filling the entire zone with a dramatic heap of tangled metalwork.

THE LEAST SATISFACTORY ELECTION

In 1986 the electors of San Mateo County, California, voted for Mr Brendan Maguire to be sheriff with an overwhelming 81,679 majority.

Only when the results were announced did anyone point out that Mr Maguire had been dead for two months.

His continuing popularity was due to his legendary performance in the 1948 Gaelic Cup Final when his side was heavily defeated by a team that included his brother.

THE LEAST SUCCESSFUL TOP SECRET

The F-19 Stealth Fighter plane was so secret that not even American senators voting for its billion-dollar development were allowed to see the plans.

It was so secret that when an F-19 crashed in the Sequoia National Park, California, the Defence Department put a news blackout on the event, stationed armed guards around the area and sent aircraft to patrol for intruders.

It was so secret that the Pentagon refused even to acknowledge the existence of the so-called 'invisible fighter'.

In July 1986 Testor Toys innocently produced a model kit for the F-19 and 100,000 children bought them in high street stores for around $10 each. When the facts were pointed out to the manufacturers, they said: 'You've got to have a bit of mystery about it. That makes it exciting.'

THE LEAST SUCCESSFUL OPENING CEREMONY

Wishing to open their new pistol range in style, officials of Brigham City decided in 1975 to invite a team of crack marksmen from the Utah Peace Force. The idea was that one of them would step forward and break the ceremonial ribbon with a single bullet.

It was a complete triumph. Five hundred bullets later the ribbon remained impressively unspoiled. According to an eyewitness, it was only cut when on officer stepped forward and 'let go with a shot gun' at point-blank range, leaving the ribbon in smouldering shreds.

POLICE TRAINING LATEST

In an attempt to train cadets in the art of interviewing robbery witnesses, officials at Albuquerque Police Academy decided in March 1975 to stage a mock break-in during an afternoon class.

The plan was that Detective David Garcia and Sergeant Robert Coon, two tutors at the academy, would dress up as an Indian and a drunk, respectively. They would then enter the class, conduct a smash-and-grab raid on the teacher, Mr Ivall Miller, and leave quickly so that cadets could practice interviewing each other about what they had seen.

Naturally, events took a very different course. The intruders had just burst into the class and were busy emptying Mr Miller's pockets when about twenty cadets stormed forward in scenes of total mayhem to lift bodily, frisk, and generally duff over the intruders. When one student identified her tutor beneath an Indian head-dress, her shouts were drowned in what had rapidly become a brawl.

Order had just been restored when Detective Garcia got up and 'shot' one of the students with blank cartridges in a gun which the crime-fighting cadets had neglected to confiscate.

'Next year we are going to have to figure out a different way to do this,' an academy official said afterwards.

THE LEAST SUCCESSFUL STATUE

In 1972 Mr W. M. Riesk of Salt Lake City commissioned a working model of Abraham Lincoln. It had 2,000 computerized parts and 300 movements, including breathing, heartbeats and a lifelike mouth through which came a speech pre-recorded by the Hollwood actor, Royal Dano.

At the start of a four-year, coast-to-coast tour of shopping precincts the statue was erected at the Northgate Centre in Seattle. A large crowd gathered round, expecting to hear Lincoln's celebrated

address, which begins: 'What is that we hold most dear amongst us? Our own liberty and prosperity.'

However, all thirty-one channels of the computer were jammed by signals from the local rock-and-roll radio station and what actually came out of the president's lips were the words:

> I wanna tell ya I can hardly speak.
> I wanna get off, mamma.
> I can hardly feel the pain no more.
> I wanna get my rocks.

Having identified this as the Rolling Stones, Mr Riesk called in an electrician from Los Angeles, who improved things no end. After twenty-one hours of work Lincoln had lost his voice altogether and was only able to breath out.

The statue continued its national tour silent and sitting still. Mr Riesk said that he was carrying on because 'I am patriotic. I even cry when I hear "The Star-Spangled Banner".'

FIVE

NEWS FROM THE REST OF THE WORLD

In which Julie Andrews is silenced; witchcraft prevails; and Freddie Frinton confuses the nation.

HOW SPECIAL ARE THE IRISH?

THE LEAST SUCCESSFUL BUS LAUNCH

With a great fanfare Bombadier (Ireland) Ltd launched 'the bus of the eighties'. The plan was to have the Irish Minister of Transport, Mr Reynolds, drive the first one out of the works on a triumphant tour of Limerick.

On 10 November 1980, he got into the bus but could not start it. Bombadier officials said the batteries were flat. New ones were fitted, but with no visible consequence. Technicians worked underneath the fine bus throughout the launching ceremony. When the minister threw the bottle of champagne he could not break it. Eventually, he hurled it with such violence that the Mayor of Limerick was drenched. 'It's all part of the risks attached to the office,' he said.

The Very Reverend Dean Emeritus M. J. Talbot prayed for the bus whereupon the minister drove out of the works hooting his horn en route to a reception at the Shamrock Hotel, Bunratty. Halfway there the bus broke down and the VIPs completed the journey by car.

In a speech applauding this fine vehicle for the new age the minister said that 'last week Mrs Reynolds and I launched a ship in Cork; there was not nearly as much excitement'.

THE ACTOR WHO KNOWS WHEN TO STOP

No actor is more exciting to watch than the mould-breaking Irish thespian, Alan Devlin. As happy off stage as on, he can inject drama into even the most lacklustre play by his ability to leave the stage in mid-performance with no warning whatsoever. His finest hour came while he was playing Sir Joseph Porter in the Dublin Gaiety Theatre's 1987 production of HMS Pinafore.

Gilbert and Sullivan's operetta was wandering to its predictable conclusion when he turned to the audience, said 'F... this for a game of soldiers, I'm going home,' clambered through the orchestra pit, shouting 'Finish it yourself' and vanished.

Still dressed in the flamboyant costume of an admiral, this excellent man went straight to Neary's bar. The cast and audience thought they had lost him for the night, but not so. Because he was still wired for sound, the evening was further enhanced by the tones of this great actor ordering a round of drinks.

Such a performance as this, however, is not given without a lengthy apprenticeship. He first went missing in 1982, muttering audible obscenities, half-way through a tedious play called *Ducking Out* at the Duke of York's Theatre in London. His stature grew yet further when he brought an early and welcome end to the vastly overlong Eugene O'Neill play *A Moon For The Misbegotten*. He was in Ireland by the time the director tracked him down.

LEAST SUCCESSFUL FIRE STATION

Roused by the alarm, the firemen of Arklow in County Wicklow raced to their posts in December 1984 only to find flames completely engulfing their own fire station. 'Christmas is always a busy time for us,' Mr Michael O'Neill, the Chief Fire Officer, said, explaining why the fire had raged unnoticed.

'The lads found their equipment and protective clothing had been destroyed and we watched the station burn to the ground,' he said philosophically. It was the second time Arklow fire station had burned down in recent years.

MORE NEWS FROM ARKLOW

Not only does this attractive resort boast a celebrated fire station, but it is also the home of the Arklow Music Festival, which hosted the least successful choral contest on 12 March 1978. Just one choir entered and even then it only managed to come second.

The Dublin Welsh Male Voice Choir failed to win first prize, the judges said, as a punishment for arriving forty-five minutes late.

The first *Book of Heroic Failures* contained a pleasantly inaccurate version of this in the chapter of 'Stories We Failed To Pin Down'. I am indebted for the new information to the choir's president, who signed himself 'Ogmore, not Mr Ogmore, or Ogmore something, it is just Ogmore'.

THE WORST BEST MAN

Choosing the right sort of best man is the key to the smooth running of a wedding ceremony. In 1920 Albert Muldoon agreed to be the best man for his good friend Christopher and what a wise choice he proved to be.

At the service in Kileter parish church Mr Muldoon wasted no time in standing on the wrong side of the groom. So, when the priest began the service he naturally addressed his questions to Albert, never having seen the happy couple before.

As Christopher was understandably nervous and tongue-tied on this great occasion, Albert answered for him. Only at the signing of the register, when the best man was putting his name under the space marked 'groom' at the priest's direction, did the bride object.

Thanks to this best man the ceremony was doubly memorable for the couple because they had to do the whole thing again.

THE LEAST SUCCESSFUL NAVIGATION

In 1938 Douglas 'Wrong Way' Corrigan was given a tickertape welcome down Broadway after flying across the Atlantic by mistake. On 16 July he boarded his nine-year-old monoplane, which cost him £150, intending to fly to Los Angeles. Onlookers at the Floyd Bennet Airfield in New York noticed, however, that, instead of turning westward as expected, he took an easterly direction shortly after take-off in thick fog.

Twenty-eight hours, thirteen minutes later, he landed at Baldonnel Aerodrome near Dublin, where the airport manager said it was 'a great day for the Irish'. On arrival, Mr Corrigan said that he was 'pretty tired', having travelled at 90 mph equipped only with a pressure gauge, a compass and a map of the United States of America. He did not take any food supplies. 'I want to do this trip again,' he told astonished reporters.

In America he was hailed as 'another Lindberg' and New York Irish groups argued for several days over the right to organize the welcoming reception. Manhattan won and gathered twenty other Corrigans, mostly policemen, to greet their namesake. Parades and speeches lasted all day.

THE RICHES OF ITALY

THE LEAST SUCCESSFUL TERRORISTS

Few urban guerillas have inspired less fear or wreaked less havoc than the Gatti Gang, who were the outstanding terrorists of their generation. A Milan-based cell of Italy's Red Brigade, they only ever had one bomb and were so scared of it that a fellow terrorist told them to 'give up. You're a danger to everyone'.

Most of their robbery plans had to be shelved because none of them could drive a car. They had to travel everywhere by bus and one bank-raid was carried out on a motor scooter. When they did stage a hold-up to raise funds for their subversive activities, they got away with 18,000 lira (£9).

All their pistols were too rusty to fire and, while trying to replace them, they were swindled out of £1,000 in an arms deal that went wrong. The group's strategy meetings often had to be postponed because the leader was nearly always suffering from a heavy cold.

The gang's finest hour came when their leader, Enrico Gatti, gave himself up and urged the other twenty-seven to throw in the towel. 'Desert,' Signor Gatti told a packed courtroom, 'it's all over. Ten years of struggle have brought us nothing but tears. Lots of our young members want to go home and live in peace.'

THEFT, ITALIAN-STYLE

Marble floors offer unique opportunities to the Italian bank robber and Carlo Colodi has explored many of them. In September 1979 he parked his car outside Milan's Banca Agricultura and dashed in with a scarf hiding his face and a revolver in his hand.

Hitting his foot on the corner of the mat, he slid across the marble floor. His scarf dropped off, revealing his face, and, as he fell, he accidentally fired his revolver. Scrambling hastily to his feet, he ran to the cashier's desk, skidded wildly and grabbed at a counter to keep his balance. To do this he had to drop the gun, whereupon, according to one Italian report, 'the entire bank rocked with hilarity'.

Rightly offended by this lack of appreciation, our man ceased his artistry, turned, ran, slipped and crawled out of the bank to find a police officer writing out a ticket for his car, which was parked in a no-waiting zone.

PACIFISM MARCHES ON

In October 1981 the pacifist composer, Luciano Berio, gave a concert of his latest work to promote peace. While conducting the open-air concert at Orvieto, he signalled for a cannon to be fired to indicate the destructive vileness of war.

The explosion was larger than planned and, when the smoke cleared, Signor Franco Ciampella, a member of the audience, was

found, bruised, bleeding and severely shocked on the ground after the blast had hurled him from his seat in the front row. Other members of the audience had minor cuts and the ambulance brigade was kept busy for hours. In the confusion fighting broke out.

'This had to happen when I'm trying to stop war with my music,' the composer said.

THE LEAST SUCCESSFUL SHIPBUILDING

Here again Italy can teach us a great deal.

Although they specialize in making smaller vessels, the Intermarine company at Ameglia amazed all Italy in 1981 by landing a £4 million contract to build one minesweeper and three military launches for the Malaysian government.

Undeterred, they set about their task. Only when the huge craft were completed did the builders recall that their shipyards were connected to the sea by the River Magra upon which nestled the attractively minute Colombiera Bridge. Not one of their new vessels was able to pass underneath it.

Intermarine offered to knock down the bridge and rebuild it, but the local council refused and the people of Ameglia gathered round to admire their new navy.

THE LEAST SUCCESSFUL WEDDING CAKE

Your wedding is a day to remember and Signor Enrico Faldini of Naples is unlikely to forget his. At the reception during 1981 the wedding cake exploded when a waiter was lighting the candles with the result that two guests, two waiters and a tourist taking a photograph of Signora Faldini were treated for shock.

Credit here goes to the chef who later said: 'I think I must have used too much alcohol in the mix.'

THE WORST RESCUE DOG

A key member of the mountain rescue team in the village of Val-chiusella in the northern Italian Alps was Bruno, a St Bernard dog with a genius for getting lost.

Bursting with enthusiasm, he always raced on ahead. Once in 1980 it took a second search party longer to recover Bruno than the climbers he was trying to find. This was the eighth time in two years that Bruno had been rescued, and the ideal moment to bring his great career to an end.

EMERGING NATIONS

THE LEAST BELLICOSE WAR

Outraged by the news that King Alfonso XII had been insulted during his state visit to Paris, the mayor of Lijar, a small town in Southern Spain, declared war on France.

While the 300 citizens backed his passionate call to arms, nobody was certain what to do next. Not a single shot was fired although the mayor, Don Miguel Garcia Saez, nonetheless became known as 'the terror of the Sierras' for this exploit.

Ninety-three years later King Juan Carlos, Alfonso's grandson, made a visit to France which went off without hitch. In 1981 the town council of Lijar decided that 'in view of the excellent attitude of the French', it would be safe to suspend hostilities.

THE LEAST SUCCESSFUL UNDERCOVER
OPERATION

Two undercover agents from the Spanish Civil Guard spent an evening in 1975 trailing three extremely suspicious-looking characters round Vittoria. At midnight they followed them into a Basque nightclub.

They crossed the dance-floor and were just going to pounce when the dubious trio sprang up, put them into half-nelsons and frog-marched them out of the building.

The three were undercover agents from the Civil Guard who had been following the other two all night on the grounds that they looked extremely suspicious.

LEAST SUCCESSFUL NEW YEAR BROADCAST

The world watches with growing admiration as Chancellor Helmut Kohl of West Germany steams ahead with pioneering work in this field. In 1987 national TV got the wrong tape and reran the speech he had given the year before. Everyone was enchanted to hear it again.

On 1 January 1988 all Germany gathered round their sets to see if it would be shown a third time. But that year things went even better. First, it was wrongly introduced as 'the Chancellor's Christmas message', whereupon the screen went blank for two minutes. When the presenter came back to correct this error, he impressed the entire nation by announcing a completely different programme. 'And now,' he said, ' "Dinner For One", Freddie Frinton's comedy sketch about an overworked butler.'

At this point Chancellor Kohl appeared and started talking about the economy.

THE LEAST SUCCESSFUL SAFE MOTORING COMPETITION

Wishing to enhance their country's reputation for careful driving, the French held a safe motoring contest in 1987. The plan was to award free petrol tokens to motorists who impressed roadside police with their respect for the law and concern for others.

After several days they had still not awarded a single prize and so the police decided to lower their standards. Hereafter they would give the tokens to any driver who was obeying the basic traffic regulations. Even this proved difficult.

When gendarmes tried to flag down the first winner, he assumed he was in trouble and raced away. When they signalled for the second winner to pull off the road, he accelerated through a red traffic light and the police had to book him instead.

In the end they gave the award to anyone they could find with a current driving licence whose car was fitted with a seat belt.

THE LEAST EFFECTIVE ELECTRIC CHAIR

As part of his vigorous campaign to modernize Abyssinia in 1890, the forward-looking Emperor Menelek II ordered three electric chairs from New York. Only when they arrived did he learn that for the very best results you need a supply of electricity, which in those days, Abyssinia lacked.

Two of the chairs were thrown out and one was used by the Emperor as his throne.

LEAST SUCCESSFUL ATTEMPT TO CONTROL FOOTBALL ROWDYISM

The powerful effects of tear gas were fully displayed in October 1987 during an African League soccer match between Gor Mahia and AFC Leopard. Trouble broke out when a Gor Mahia official went onto the pitch and refused to leave it, despite complaints from the opposition that he was using witchcraft to influence the game.

In the confusion which followed, twenty-two players, eight members of the training staff and a large section of the crowd joined a fist-swinging free-for-all on the pitch. Taking firm action, the police raced on with tear gas, but were themselves overwhelmed and had to be carried off by the team, having made no arrests. Witchcraft prevailed and Gor Mahia won 1–0.

THE LEAST SATISFACTORY PERFORMANCE OF *THE SOUND OF MUSIC*

Only the South Koreans have really got to grips with *The Sound of Music*, the well-known film in which Julie Andrews and a selection of carbolically scrubbed infants burst into song up Alps, inside monasteries, on assorted staircases and in a wide range of wholly surprising locations.

Finding the film a shade overlong, the Koreans wisely decided to cut out all the songs. Shown with no music whatsoever, yet still called *The Sound of Music*, the film proved extremely popular and played to full houses all over South-East Asia.

THE MOST CHAOTIC COURT CASE

A total of 153 Greek immigrants appeared at the Central Court, Sydney in June 1978, accused of mass deception, forging medical certificates, claiming incorrect pensions and defrauding the Commonwealth. Hardly any of them spoke English.

Many were unable to get into the courtroom because the entrance was barricaded by a demonstration of social workers protesting in support of the Greek Community.

When the case eventually started more than thirty lawyers squeezed into Number Three Court where hundreds of defendants, relatives and friends so crowded the place that some barristers were unable to reach the bench at all. Further confusion occurred when the judge discovered that none of the charges on the court sheet bore any resemblance to his own numbered papers.

When the judge called the first case, Clive Evatt QC rose to his feet and was unable to pronounce the name of his client.

Meanwhile, Mr T. P. Griffin, for the Crown Solicitor, told the judge he did not appear to have any papers relating to the man Mr Evatt was representing.

'Well, if you ever do find the papers would you give me a telephone call?' Mr Evatt replied.

Yet more confusion followed when two other lawyers found that they had both been briefed to represent the same man. The defendant was asked to settle the dispute, whereupon the winning solicitor gave a boxer's victory salute and then discovered that he had never seen the man before. It transpired that there were two defendants with the same name.

After seventeen minutes without progress in the first case the judge adjourned the hearing for three months on the grounds that it would take that long to sort out.

SIX

THE INCREDIBLE WORLD OF CRIME

In which a Russian burglar turns musical; short-sight saves a Chinese take-away manager; and 63 varieties of sulphur-crested parrot get a surprise.

THE GANG WHO GOT LOST

At 5 a.m. on September 1981 the Edmonton Two raided the Petro-Canada fuel station in Vancouver, locked the attendant in the washroom and made their getaway with a hundred dollars. Coming from Edmonton, they did not know their way around Vancouver and twenty minutes later they drove up at the same petrol station to ask directions.

The attendant, Mr Karnail Dhillon, had just escaped from the washroom and so was alarmed to see the burly pair approaching the cashier's window again. 'They wanted me to tell them the way to Port Moody,' he said. 'I guess they didn't recognize me or the station.'

He was just calling the police when the pair came back yet again to say they could not get their car started. Learning that a mechanic would not be on duty until 8 a.m., they went back to the car and ran the battery down trying to start it. They were on the phone to a towing company when they were arrested by Police Constable Tom Drechsel.

THE LEAST SUCCESSFUL SAFE-BREAKERS

Using the latest sophisticated equipment, a gang from Chichester set about cutting open a safe at the Southern Leisure Centre. Happily, it was the wrong sophisticated equipment and in no time they had welded up the door. The manager said that after their good work the safe was so secure that it took three hours to open using hammer and chisel.

THE LEAST SUCCESSFUL JEWELLERY RAID

With a thoughtfulness that is rare nowadays, Paul Lassis alerted the staff of a Bristol jewellery shop to his forthcoming raid by sounding his car horn loudly, while driving up on the pavement outside.

With the entire staff watching, he reached out to smash the shop window. As his hammer bounced harmlessly off the toughened glass, he tried to reverse his car through it, but missed, crashed over a wastepaper bin and was stuck fast when a passing evangelical missionary, Mr Herbert Eaton, prevented a getaway by hurling his bicycle through the car's windscreen.

THE LEAST SUCCESSFUL CAR THEFT

While parked in 1987 outside the garage of Mr Colin Baggs, a suspected car thief, two policemen had allowed their windows to steam up. Having gained no evidence whatsoever to support their case, they were just on the point of giving up when Mr Baggs broke into their vehicle.

The immortal Baggs was himself unable to explain this moment of brilliance, but admiring members of Frome magistrates bench described it as 'a classic own goal'.

THE LEAST SUCCESSFUL ARMED ROBBERY

Few armed robbers have taken a more original approach to their calling than the innovator who held up Mohammed Razaq's grocery store in Wandsworth on 20 July 1979. Bursting in from Felsham Road, he said: 'Give me the money from your till or I will shoot.'

Even in moments of high drama Mr Razaq prides himself on his eye for detail. 'Where is your gun?' he asked. At this point the great innovator had to reply that he didn't actually have a gun, but if there were any further difficulties he would go out, get one and come back. Having made this point, he left.

THE LEAST SUCCESSFUL CRIME PREVENTION

When his nightly stroll brought him face to face with a mugging, a young Brisbane doctor felt he had no alternative but to intervene. Seeing, in May 1982, a robust man struggling brutally with an old lady crying for help in the street, he cried 'Stop at once', and leaped forward, grabbing her assailant by the shoulders.

He had laid into the surprised mugger and was generally man-handling him, when the director of the television drama for which this was an outdoor sequence stepped forward to protect his cast.

THE MOST NOTICEABLE BURGLAR

So few house-breakers give genuine pleasure and entertainment. In February 1981 a young Soviet burglar broke into a flat at Baku on the Caspian Sea, while the owners were away on holiday. Exhausted by all the looting, he ran himself a soothing hot bath and then sat down to pour himself a couple of vodkas. Feeling peckish, he knocked up a little something to eat.

Thoroughly relaxed, he poured another vodka, strolled over to the upright and started playing Grieg's Piano Concerto. After the resounding C major sforzando chord he was just starting the an-imato section, and bursting into song (although strictly speaking no words were actually written for the piece), when the police arrived, alerted by the complaints of several philistine neighbours.

THE MOST IGNORED ROBBER

While waiting for his girlfriend in West Croydon, Mr David Morris devised a foolproof scheme to get rich quick without saying a word. All he would have to do was march into any local shop and hold up a fearsome sheet of paper bearing the message: 'I have a gun in my pocket. I will shoot if you do not hand over the money.' In February 1986 he put it to the test.

When he went into the chemist's, the female assistant thought it was an obscene note and refused to read it. At the Asian shop next door the owner gazed blankly at the words, shook his head and said that he couldn't read English. And at the Chinese take-away the manager announced that he did not have his glasses. It was while supposedly searching for them in the backroom that he called the police who put an end to what could have been an extremely promising career.

THE DANISH DIMENSION, PART ONE

In June 1987 three enterprising Danish robbers worked long and hard trying to dynamite open a safe at the bank in Munkebo, Denmark. Despite detonating six times the required amount of dynamite, they found that the safe remained firmly closed. They did, however, demolish the bank and the explosion was reported ten miles away.

THE DANISH DIMENSION, PART TWO

Racing out of a Copenhagen bank in 1978, a Danish thief flagged down a police car. Thinking it was a taxi because it had a light on

81

top, he jumped in the back with a sackful of money and shouted out his home address.

When the bank manager rushed out seeking a policeman to catch this thief, his task could not have been easier.

THE BURGLAR WHO WENT TOO FAR

A trail-blazing burglar broke into a vast mansion on millionaire's row in June 1982 at Bel Air, Los Angeles. While on a sack-filling tour of this palatial structure, he went through the ballroom into the hall, down the escalators to the single-lane swimming arbour, up to the library across the dining-room, out of the annexe and into the conservatory containing sixty-three varieties of tropical plant and a cageful of sulphur-crested parrots.

Deciding that now was the time to make a quick exit, he went back through the dining-room, up to the gymnasium across the indoor tennis-court, down a spiral staircase to an enclosed patio with synchronized fountains, out to the cocktail lounge through junior's sound-proofed drum studio and back into the room full of increasingly excited parrots who normally see nobody from one day to the next.

Panicking slightly, he ran back towards the library, through swing doors into a gallery containing the early works of Jackson Pollock, out through the kitchen across a jacuzzi enclosure and up two flights of stairs, at which point he became hysterical, ran outside along the balcony around the circular corridors, up more stairs, down the landing into the master bedroom and woke up the owners to ask them how to get out.

In order to spare him further distress, they arranged for a local policeman to escort him from the premises.

BURGLING THE WRONG PLACE

Under cover of night Vincent Pattison rowed across Regents Canal in London and broke into the wrong warehouse. Anyone could have done this: it required no special skill. However, faced with this situation, a duller man might have gone outside and broken into the correct building.

Not so Mr Pattison who started sledge-hammering through the wall. Who knows how this promising crime might have developed had not a police car drawn up outside to investigate the impressive din?

Giving up all hope of total demolition, our hero jumped back onto his boat, whereupon it sank and he had to swim to the opposite shore and hide in a nearby block of flats. The police chase ended when Mr Pattison sneezed.

THE EASIEST CRIMES TO DETECT

The greatest crimes are marked by a logic and a dazzling simplicity that enables them to be detected almost as soon as they have been committed.

In 1978, for example, Allan Bonds and Bernard Redfearn of Stoke-on-Trent stole a water tank, but forgot that it was still half-full. They left a trail of puddles and got home minutes before the police.

An American robber, Homer Lawyer, held up a bank in Miami. He pushed a note across the counter demanding cash and then fled with a sackful. It was the bank manager who noticed that he had helpfully written his name and address on the back of the note.

Kenneth Peverley made the most of the latest technology, while burgling an office in Cardiff, when he knocked over a dictating machine, which switched itself on. He was arrested when police recognized him muttering on the tape.

All the above, however, are entirely eclipsed by Mr Clive Bunyan who raided the village store at Cayton, Yorkshire, in 1970, wearing a crash helmet with the words 'CLIVE BUNYAN' written in large gold letters across the front – a definitive performance.

STEALING THE WRONG THING

With a daring that many of their older colleagues could hardly equal, two teenagers broke into a Yeovil grocery shop in April 1984.

Messrs Knibbs and Hunt located what they thought was the cash-box, wrenched it from the wall and escaped into the street. When the box started up a shrill buzzing they threw it to the ground and stamped on it, but to no avail. Despite all their efforts to stop the noise this enterprising duo finally had to dump the box in the river. They had stolen the burglar alarm.

CRIME BUSTERS

In July 1985 four West London criminals made extensive plans to rob the manager of the White Knight Laundry in Kensal Road as he left the bank with a box full of staff wages. The police were, however, tipped off and they too made extensive plans to catch them in the act.

Both parties were stationed outside Barclays bank in Chamberlayne Road, Kensal Rise and the manager was inside with a specially emptied box. As he stepped through the door, everybody was just about to act when another thief dashed out from a doorway, snatched the empty box and disappeared without trace.

PROMPT POLICE ACTION

West Midlands police moved swiftly on 15 May 1983 when a caller rang to say there was an abandoned safe on a grass verge at Halesowen. In no time a uniformed officer was on the scene, where he stood guard for over an hour until the arrival of detectives who dusted it for fingerprints.

This done, they tried taking the safe back to the police station. When all attempts at lifting it failed, the uniformed branch sent a team of constables to help, but even they could not budge it so the traffic division sent a Landrover with towing gear. Man and machine united for twenty minutes of fruitless constabulary shoving.

'That,' said an officer, 'was when we realized it was a Midlands Electricity Board junction box concreted into the ground.'

HOW TO CATCH A BLACKMAILER

In February 1988 an anonymous caller rang the police to say that he would leave poisoned chocolate bars all over Lincolnshire if they did not deposit £50,000 in the phone box at the village of Harpswell.

Sensing an easy arrest, the police left this sum in a briefcase and retired to lie in wait. At the appointed time they sprang from the bushes and pounced on an innocent villager who had come from the local caravan park to telephone his mother. In their enthusiasm to frogmarch him off to justice, they forgot their briefcase and so returned to find that the real blackmailer had now taken it.

Seeing a distant figure, the police dashed off and arrested a second blameless villager as he walked across a field to the nearby local social club.

After six hours of cross-examination the Regional Crime Squad said he had been the 'unfortunate victim of circumstance'.

THE GREAT ESCAPES

There have been three major prison escapes of interest to us in the past decade.

In the first, Tonino Lacordia cleared the wall of Madonna Del Freddo jail in August 1980, but sprained his ankle when landing and hobbled into deepest countryside. After several miles he knocked at the door of a remote cottage. The door was opened by the very policeman who had arrested him some weeks earlier and who had rented this place for a holiday to get away from it all.

In the second, two men escaped from Guelph Correctional Centre in February 1981. They climbed the fence, sprinted down the main road and dived for cover in the Colonel John McCrae Legion Hall, where more than a hundred correctional officers from the Centre were attending a seminar.

Not recognizing the staff training officer, Mr Bill Dick, the prisoners asked if he could call them a cab and they were surprised when simultaneously arrested by thirty-seven familiar warders.

In the third case, a man got out of Northeye Prison in 1981 by hiding underneath a van full of vegetables. After an invigorating ride through the Sussex countryside the van turned a corner and came to a halt. When the van had been unloaded and the warders had all gone, the prisoner crawled out to find he was now in Lewes prison.

THE LEAST SUCCESSFUL GETAWAYS

A bankrobber in Malta set a new world best when he raided the Bank of Valetta, held up the staff, seized the cash, rushed out, dashed across the road and waited at the bus stop. After fifteen minutes, with no bus in sight, he was arrested by a passing policeman whose suspicions were aroused by the 3,000 new banknotes he was clasping to his chest.

And in 1976 Mr Alfred Rivera showed the importance of split-second timing. After he had robbed a bar in San Fernando he dashed out and sprinted down the road to a prearranged meeting place where he was knocked over by his own getaway car.

SEVEN

DOING IT AT WORK

In which the King of Norway is surrounded by coconuts; a Tibetan rain-
bucket proves extremely unpopular; and
goblins are shocked in Santa's grotto.

THE LEAST SUCCESSFUL ANNUAL CONFERENCE

The British Association of Travel Agents held an outstanding annual conference at Sorrento in 1985. Delegates from Britain had already been doing solid work: the conference train was delayed by points failure at Purley; the flight was late; there was fog at Gatwick; most people arrived a day late; so many went down with food poisoning the ABTA doctor was singled out for special praise in the closing address; two fell down a marble staircase; and the marketing director of Kuoni travel developed septicaemia following a snake bite.

Furthermore, organizers of the annual golf tournament arrived to find there wasn't a golf course in Sorrento so this popular event had to be held in Dublin.

However, it was the Italian genius which brought this conference to a climax. Surrounded by marching bands and ceremonial guards, the Minister for Development addressed all the delegates in the forum at Pompeii. At this point a local travel agent, Lucio Aponte, decided this would be the ideal moment to fly overhead and drop 3,500 roses on the visitors.

The ceremony had just begun when a light aircraft appeared, swooped down, drowned out the minister, dropped the roses and missed the forum completely. Minutes later it reappeared, flying even lower and causing the delegates to crouch. Five times he flew past and five times he missed the target. Not a single flower landed near the delegates, but there were roses all over Mount Vesuvius.

LEAST SUCCESSFUL NURSE

While serving on the wards of King's College Hospital, London in 1987, a student nurse saw a frail, elderly woman seated upon the edge of a bed. 'Time for your bath,' said the good nurse. 'I've already had one,' replied the old woman who showed signs of confusion.

With kindly firmness she led the old woman to her bath, took off her clothes and washed her thoroughly. On returning to the ward, the nurse said, 'Someone else has got into your bed.' 'It's my sister,' replied the old lady. 'I've come to visit her.'

SPECIAL AWARD FOR THE POST OFFICE

After a long and expensive advertising campaign the Great British people were still glowingly unacquainted with their postcodes. In desperation the Post Office decided to launch a quiz in September 1985. There was only one question and to get a prize you merely had to get your own postcode right.

Happily, few of the replies got through. When giving their address the Post Office got their own postal code wrong. 'It was a printing error,' said the head postmaster, modestly declining to bask in the glory.

THE LEAST SUCCESSFUL SOUND EFFECT

In 1944 King Haakon of Norway delivered a rousing wartime address to his beleagured people on the BBC World Service. As His Royal Highness was running forty seconds short, the producer sent to the library for a fanfare to round things off. At this point the talk came brilliantly alive.

Haakon had just commended his country to God, made a few Nordic farewell grunts and laid down his script, when the air was suddenly alive with the sound of roundabouts and ribaldry and cockneys shouting, 'Roll up, roll up ladies and gentlemen.' The library had sent a funfair. Afterwards, the king said it was 'the sort of thing that happens'.

LEAST SUCCESSFUL WEATHER FORECAST

At the end of a bravura weather forecast in October 1987 Mr
Michael Fish told British televiewers that 'a woman rang to say
she'd heard there was a hurricane on the way. Well, don't worry.
There isn't'. Brushing aside this fanciful amateur forecast with a
chuckle, the immortal Fish predicted 'sea breezes' and a 'showery air-
flow'.

In no time Britain was hit by 120 mph winds that ripped up 300
miles of power cables, plunged a quarter of the country into darkness, blocked 200 roads with fallen branches, felled 25 per cent of
the trees in Kent and stopped all rail traffic in the south of England
for twenty-four hours. An ambulance at Hayling Island was hit by a
yacht floating across the road and the Meteorological Office said it
was the worst hurricane since 1703.

A spokesman for Mr Fish later said: 'It is really all a question of
detail.'

THE LEAST SUCCESSFUL SALVAGE OPERATION

In 1983 an Icelandic salvage firm announced that it had located the
wreck of the *Wapen Van Amsterdam*, a Dutch treasure ship which
sank in 1667 with forty crates of gold and four tons of uncut
diamonds on board. The government gave £1 million to raise it
and workers burrowed twenty feet beneath the ocean bed. Iceland
was aflame with excitement.

On the great day crowds formed, children waved flags and fleets
of official limousines arrived from Reykjavik. Eventually, through
the waves appeared something more extraordinary than even they
could have expected: a German trawler which sank in 1903 with a
consignment of herrings.

IMPRESSIVE WORK AT THE SAFETY EXECUTIVE

The Health and Safety Executive was set up in 1974 to check safety standards in the workplace. In 1987 staff at the London office went on strike because their headquarters were 'unsafe'.

'This place is a death trap,' said Mr Don Street, a union spokesman. During renovation work at the Notting Hill headquarters his members faced a daily barrage of flying glass and falling masonry, tripping headlong over electricity cables and colliding with workmen carrying planks round corners.

The *pièce de résistance* came when scaffolding fell through a glass roof and crashed on to a clerk's desk.

THE LEAST PERCEPTIVE REVIEW

The most important book review in our field was penned by Mr Ed Zern of *Field and Stream*. In the 1950s he told his editor that the countryside magazine would benefit from a books department.

Impressed by this idea, the editor commissioned him to select a good outdoor book and review it. Missing the point with a wholeheartedness that borders on genius, Mr Zern chose *Lady Chatterley's Lover* which, unknown to him, had been banned throughout the Commonwealth and tried for obscenity because of the unending scenes of outdoor carnality involving the gamekeeper and his employer's wife.

Mr Zern's review was a masterpiece of the genre:

> Although written many years ago, *Lady Chatterley's Lover* has just been reissued by Grove Press, and this fictional account of the day-by-day life of an English gamekeeper is still of considerable interest to outdoor-minded readers, as it contains many passages on pheasant-raising, the apprehending of poachers, ways to control vermin, and other chores and duties of the

professional gamekeeper. Unfortunately, one is obliged to wade through many pages of extraneous material in order to discover and savour these sidelights on the management of a Midland shooting estate, and in this reviewer's opinion this book cannot take the place of J. R. Miller's *Practical Gamekeeping*.

LEAST SUCCESSFUL ARCHAEOLOGICAL DISCOVERY

In one of the most exciting archaeological finds of the century a team of researchers in Tehran uncovered the skeleton of a dinosaur which had hitherto only been found in North America.

The ribs and vertebrae were carefully preserved and in 1930 a scientific mission from Madrid flew out to conduct a thorough examination.

Things got even more exciting when their final report announced that the reptile was, in fact, an abandoned hay-making machine which had been caught in a landslide.

THE WORST MECHANIC

The US Navy launched an inquiry in 1987 to find the identity of a mechanic at Jacksonville Air Depot who singlehandedly caused 300 jets to be grounded. 'We were told he was simply not mechanically inclined,' a spokesman for the Naval Office in Washington said. 'For years this guy was taking these gearboxes apart, then putting them back together – with parts left over when he was done.'

Although there were no serious mishaps, there were constant technical hitches as a result of his modifications to the planes.

Ten Navy engineerng teams were dispatched worldwide and a bulletin ordered anyone flying these aircraft to see if the maintenance records were signed 'Wood', 'Woods', or illegible. The A-4 Skyhawk, the A-6 Intruder Attack plane and the EA-6B Prowler electronic warfare plane were all grounded.

THE EXPOSÉ THAT BACKFIRED

Strong candidates in this category are the two ace reporters from the *Independent*, who attempted to expose the shadowy world of private detectives.

Adopting fictitious identities they approached several sleuths asking them to spy on their own editor. Even though the detectives inhabit a shadowy world, they were so horrified by the suggestion that they decided to expose their would-be exposers.

Every move of the two journalists, who stationed themselves in a London hotel, was carefully monitored by a swarm of private eyes – two of whom posed as a liftboy and a chambermaid. Eventually, they found out everything about the reporters, including the fact that they at first forgot to pay for the thirty-eight mini-bar drinks consumed during the assignment.

When one of the newshounds went to the hotel lobby at lunch-time to use a telephone, he was 'almost squashed in the rush of half a dozen investigators racing for the booth next to him', according to one of the detectives.

The journalists' exposé appeared the next day. In the following Sunday's *Observer* they were able to read the detectives' detailed exposé of the shadowy world of journalism.

THE SLOWEST-SELLING POSTCARD

The world's slowest-selling postcard depicts a fascinating fourteenth-century Tibetan rain-bucket.

The inspired publications officer at the Victoria & Albert Museum had 5,000 copies of this exquisite card printed. Of these 24 were destroyed in a flood and 4,972 are still available. Only four were ever sold . . .

THE LEAST SUCCESSFUL SANTA CLAUS

In 1983 happy children had just left Santa's grotto amidst much yo-ho-hoing when police walked in, clapped Father Christmas in handcuffs and frog-marched him out through the toy department at Allders store in Croydon. Amazed goblins who assist in the grotto said that Santa was 'taken to the police station and charged with persistent non-payment of traffic fines'.

THE LEAST SUCCESSFUL NEWSPAPER COMPETITION

In May 1986 the distinguished British journalist Henry Porter revealed that he had planted five deliberate grammatical errors in his *Sunday Times* column and would send a bottle of champagne to any reader who spotted them all correctly.

Letters poured in by the sackload. The next week Mr Porter announced that readers had found not one of the five mistakes. However, they had located a further 23 of which he was not aware.

This overtakes the previous best. In 1964 the *Carmel Independent* in California printed a school photograph and asked readers to identify which child became a well-known celebrity. While cropping the picture for publication, an enthusiastic sub-editor cut out the child in question, making it impossible to win the contest from merely looking at the paper.

EIGHT

MAKING THE MOST OF YOUR FREE TIME

In which killer tomatoes go berserk in San
Diego; three famous explorers get lost;
and thirty-two intrepid moles turn up.

THE LEAST SUCCESSFUL HOME REPAIRS

Home repairs offer immense scope to the right sort of person. In 1980 Mr Brian Heise of Utah showed the way when he woke to find a burst pipe flooding his house.

Deciding to hire a pump, he went out to his car only to find that a tyre was flat. Returning indoors to make a phone call, he received an electric shock so great that he was hurled across the room and ripped the telephone out of the wall.

He then found that dampness had caused the floor to swell and the front door was jammed so he could not get out. A seminal figure in the world of home repairs, he spent some while screaming through the window for help. Only when a neighbour smashed down the front door did Mr Heise notice that his car had been stolen.

Having informed the police, hired a pump, sealed the leak and cleaned up his flat, Mr Heise felt that the moment had come to relax. Displaying an impressive versatility, he went to a nearby civil war pageant and within minutes of arrival sat on a bayonet.

LEAST SUCCESSFUL ATTEMPT TO CLEAR MOLEHILLS

Tired of the ten large molehills that flourished on his lawn, Mr Oscar Ejiamike decided to remove them. After a vigorous campaign of bombing, gassing and waiting round in the dark with a raised shovel he found that the ten molehills survived intact. There were also twenty-two new ones.

At this point our man decided to 'surprise the moles' with a midnight poisoning raid. In May 1984 he drove his Jaguar 2.4 Automatic to the edge of the lawn and trained the headlamps upon the enemy zone. While reaching across for the poison, Mr Ejiamike knocked the car into reverse and accelerated through the wall of his cottage, knocking over the electric heater, bursting his petrol tanks, setting fire to his newly decorated sitting room, and wrecking his car.

While this certainly surprised the moles, it had no effect upon the thirty-two molehills. Next morning Mr Ejimike bought twenty-two bags of ready-mixed cement and announced that he was going to concrete the lawn over.

THE WORST FILMS

In the history of the cinema the World's Worst Film Festival proved a highspot. Delegates in 1980 to this treasure-house of special cel-luloid moments got off to a cracking start with *Tiny Town*, the world's first all-midget western. It mainly consisted of cowboys walking under saloon doors, chasing each other under bar-room tables and riding into the sunset on what were obviously Shetland ponies. Applause broke out in the chase sequence when the three-foot-nine-inch hero 'Rocky' Curtis pursued the three-foot-eight-inch villain Little Billy. Rocky galloped out of town on a black horse, and was next seen scooting along on a white one, only to arrive at his ranch reunited with the black one.

For six days the festival maintained this high standard and special acclaim went to *The Attack of The Killer Tomatoes*, a four-hour epic in which a consignment of giant tomatoes goes berserk and terror-izes San Diego. In one of the best scenes a housewife is threatened by a bloodthirsty seedless oozing out of her in-sink garbage-grinding unit.

The eventual winner was *They Saved Hitler's Brain* in which the Führer's grey cells wreak post-bunker havoc on a scale that would have surprised even Adolf.

THE LEAST SUCCESSFUL CAMPING INSTRUCTIONS

Few campsites are blessed with such comprehensive regulations as Camping Atlanta at Lungomare Sud in Italy.

After the general instruction that 'cars must enter or go away from the camp with motors out' we reach the all-embracing rule 15, which reads

THEN IS STRICTLY FORBIDDEN TO:

a) Reserve box parking, spaces with chairs, fences, rape or other means

b) Dainage of the plants and equiman

c) Not teak paper other box

d) Dig simples around tents

e) Play with ball of tamboury in the camp

g) Set to go into the camp, not autorized from the direction

So that campers know exactly where they stand, rule 17 concludes: 'The above listed rules are inappellable. All of the camping personnel are authorized to send away anyone who does follow them.'

THE LEAST ACCURATE MAP

Few maps offer the adventurous walker quite such varied terrain as the one for the Dales National Park. Described as 'definitive' when it came out in 1969, the map contains a network of footpaths more challenging than anything previously published.

In no time keen ramblers found that one footpath went straight up a cliff face, another passed through the middle of a hospital ward and a third involved crossing the River Ribble in two places without the benefit of a bridge.

In an enthusiastic report the *Guardian* newspaper said that 'any walker determined to follow the line would have had to wade across the river up to his neck, walk for 200 metres along the eastern bank, and then wade back again'.

THE LEAST SUCCESSFUL DO-IT-YOURSELF EXPERT

An ever popular field, DIY has produced an astonishing crop of cult figures. Supreme in this category is Mr Antony Drew of Kent who showed the way with his imaginative attempt to renew a shower curtain.

Sensing the untold possibilities of a ladder, he managed in a single manoeuvre to fall off and splinter the bath enamel, while his hammer cracked the bath and his drill smashed the basin. Resting briefly, he went downstairs to repair the fireplace and poked his hammer through the TV screen before returning to his real favourite, the ladder.

Moving outside, he climbed it once more to paint the bathroom window. With adult consistency he fell off again. This time his chisel flew through the window and cracked the lavatory bowl, while Mr Drew himself went hurtling through the roof of his carport.

But for sheer elegant simplicity surely no one can beat Michael Taylor of Gloucester who decided to lower the floor of his cellar and make it an extra room. He dug away the foundations and the entire building collapsed.

THE LEAST SUCCESSFUL ATTEMPT TO RAISE MONEY FOR CHARITY

In 1986 Mr Jeffrey Gill decided to raise £1,000 for the Bude coast-guards by windsurfing from the North Devon coast to Lundy Island.

When, several hours later, there was no sign of him, the coast-guards launched a full-scale air-sea rescue operation involving the Bristol channel lifeboat, the Lundy ferry, the Bude inflatable life-raft, a helicopter from RAF Chivenor and mobile coastguard units from as far away as Cornwall. The total cost of the operation was £2,000, exactly twice what he had hoped to raise.

Eventually, he was found, substantially becalmed and floating towards America. 'The wind dropped and my flares didn't work,' said Mr Gill, who runs a shop in Widemouth Bay called Outdoor Adventure.

THE MOST POINTLESS PETITION

In this genre the great A. N. Wilson is unsurpassed. During the autumn of 1987 the contemporary novelist became enraged that Poets' Corner in Westminster Abbey had no memorial bust honouring Matthew Arnold.

With a faultless display of campaigning skills, he fired off letters pointing out this disgraceful neglect and organized a petition of right-thinking literati, headed by the biographer Victoria Glendinning and Auberon Waugh, the editor of the *Literary Review*.

In a crusading editorial, Mr Waugh wrote that 'unlike many of those whose monuments adorn the abbey, Arnold's reputation has stood the test of time, and continued exclusion seems shameful'. He urged his readers to write immediately to the Right Reverend Dean of Westminster, who was instantly submerged in a barrage of irate mail.

The campaign reached the perfect conclusion when the Dean wrote back thanking them for their interest and pointing out that their proposal seemed to overlook the extremely lifelike bust of Arnold which had been in the Abbey since 1891.

THE WORST COUGH

In 1988 Alan Parkes of Sydney had what is widely thought to be the most troublesome cough in modern history. His constant hacking in the middle of the night terrified the woman next door who woke up and thought it was gunfire. Assuming there was a crazed gunman on the loose, she barricaded herself into her bedroom and called the police.

Minutes later armed officers poured in from all over Sydney, including members of a crack 'tactical response group'. Within half an hour they had surrounded Alan's house and taken up siege postures in readiness for a shoot-out.

With marksmen crouching right round the suburb, their leader knocked on the door. When it opened and our man stood there choking in winter-weight pyjamas, neither party could believe what they were seeing. Mr Parkes, who is a council tip worker, promised to get some lozenges.

THE LEAST SUCCESSFUL FISHING TRIP

It was the perfect day for fishing. Leaving his farm on the North Kent coast one bright Thursday in August 1981, Mr John Jenkins took his family to the nearby resort of Seasalter.

Three-quarters of a mile out onto the mudflats his four-wheel-drive Dodge got stuck. Mr Jenkins made the long trek back to a telephone and called out one of his tractors. As soon as it arrived this got stuck as well. The family climbed out and watched as the tide covered both vehicles.

On the Friday morning the first tractor was pulled out by a second. Together they set off to rescue the Dodge, but *en route* both got stuck and were engulfed by the incoming tide.

Mr Jenkins now had three vehicles under water and so set out with his third tractor to remedy the situation. In rescuing the Dodge this tractor also became stuck and that night it too disappeared beneath the waves.

By Saturday morning word had spread of this great sea adventure and whole families travelled out across the mud to watch a mechanical digger arrive and release one tractor before itself becoming wedged in the mud. By Saturday night that was under water as well. One Sunday morning the rescued tractor went back to assist whereupon it became immediately stuck in the mud and the tide covered the entire contents of Mr Jenkins' garage.

THE LEAST SUCCESSFUL GAS CONVERSION

Since converting his orange Volvo to gas power for reasons of economy, Mr Tony Forward proudly said he had enjoyed two years of trouble-free motoring. In that time he had only once experienced any kind of bother with it.

In the early hours of a morning in 1981 there was a loud explosion which had woken not only him, but also the entire population of Derby Green, a small hamlet in Hampshire. Thinking it might be a thunderbolt, he went outside to find that the blast from his car had destroyed his garage and conservatory, scattered his freezer and its contents over the garden, blown a hole in a neighbour's garage, damaging their car, and left a fence and his own personally modified Volvo in flames. Such was the heat that a spare gas cylinder on the back seat went up and sent the roof of his car flying through the air and crashing through trees into a garden across the road.

Apart from this one incident Mr Forward experienced no trouble at all.

GREAT MOMENTS IN THE HISTORY OF EXPLORATION

Three celebrated explorers were invited to dinner at the Geographical Club in London.

Sir Vivian Fuchs had explored Greenland and East Africa and led the Commonwealth Trans-Antarctic Expedition of 1955–8.

Dr John Hemming was director of the Royal Geographical Society and a member of the 1961 Brazilian Expedition.

Robin Hanbury-Tenison had crossed South America in a small boat and explored the Indonesian islands, Ecuador, Brazil, Venezuela and the mountains of Southern Sahara as well as travelling up Africa and down the Amazon in a hovercraft.

They met at the Royal Geographical Society, just a quarter of a mile from their final destination. Within a mere fifteen minutes they were spectacularly lost in the back streets of Kensington.

THE WORST DRIVER (MALE)

The world record for the most traffic offences in the shortest period of time is held by a man from Frisco in Texas who achieved this feat in the first twenty minutes of car ownership.

Having hitch-hiked to the nearby city of McKinney on 15 October 1966, he bought a 1953 Ford and drove out of the used-car showroom at 3.50 p.m.

At 3.54 he collided with a 1952 Chevrolet driven by a local woman, Mrs Wilma Smith Bailey, at the corner of McKinney and Heard Street.

One minute later he collided again 90 feet south of Virginia

Street and Tennessee Street with another Chevrolet, driven by Miss Sally Whitsel of Farmersville.

Feeling more confident now in his new vehicle, he next drove round the courthouse one-way system in the wrong direction. Forty-six feet later he hit a 1963 Ford. It was still only 3.58.

He continued in this vein until 4.15 p.m. when he was in deep conversation with Patrolman Richard Buchanan, having just hit a Ford Mustang in Louisiana Street.

In the space of just twenty minutes he had acquired ten traffic tickets, caused six accidents, hit four cars without stopping and driven on the wrong side of the road four times.

When questioned, this determined motorist, who had not driven for ten years, said: 'They don't drive like they used to.'

THE LEAST SUCCESSFUL BIRDWATCHERS

In November 1986 200 birdwatchers from all over Britain gathered in the Scilly Isles to see the arrival of an extremely rare grey-cheeked thrush. During the long wait they discussed the bird's North African habitat, its exquisite colouring and the precise detail of its unusually melodious call.

Peering through binoculars, they saw the priceless bird fly in amidst exclamations regarding its beauty. As soon as it landed on the campsite at St Mary's Garrison Mrs S. Burrows' cat, Muffin, dashed out, snatched the thrush in its mouth, disappeared into a bush and brought the birdwatching session to a close.

THE WOMAN WHO COULDN'T ORGANIZE
A PISS-UP IN A BREWERY

In the 1970s a woman reporter, working for the *Daily Mirror*, was chided by her colleagues that she couldn't organize a piss-up in a brewery. Piqued by this comment, she announced that the following week contained her birthday and she would be arranging a party at the Fullers Brewery in Chiswick.

With a touch of sheer brilliance, she put the wrong day on the noticeboard and revellers turned up twenty-four hours early.

NINE

THE IMPORTANCE OF INDIVIDUALISM

In which an aviator studies the ostrich egg; an astronomer models himself on a kangaroo; and a traveller sleeps with a bat.

THE MOST KNOCKED OUT BOXER

The boxing ring contains no greater star than Bruce 'The Mouse' Strauss who has been knocked out more times than anybody else. He has hit the canvas on thirty-one occasions at twenty-nine locales. 'A couple of places liked me so much they asked me back for more,' says Strauss, whom grateful boxers have queued up to fight for over a decade.

The most frequently defeated pugilist in the world, Mouse explains that he is 'not competitive' and 'never got an emotional charge when the referee raised my hand'. As *Boxing News* said, this fine man 'knows the agony of victory and the thrill of defeat'.

According to his sparring partner, Richie Segedin, Mouse sometimes goes too far. 'Mouse always goes too far actually. I've seen him drink a beer that a fan offered him – during the fight. And he tries to chat up round-card girls while they walk around the ring.' Once, when knocked out, he feigned extensive injury so that he could stay in hospital for two months and court a nurse who later became Mrs Mouse.

In 1986 Strauss, who is twenty-one, twenty-eight or thirty-five depending on who's asking, says he rang the Associated Press Agency to announce his retirement, but they had 'absolutely no interest'.

Part of Strauss's record-breaking achievement is due to the fact that he fought an astronomical number of professional bouts, two of them on the same night and many under an assumed name or disguised with dyed hair or a false moustache.

THE MOST POINTLESS BY-ELECTION

We are still waiting for the definitive by-election at which no candidates poll any votes at all. But the great Gatting contest of 1816 comes close.

THE IMPORTANCE OF INDIVIDUALISM

The constituency only had three voters: Sir Mark Wood, his son (who had gone missing) and the butler, Jennings. All was peaceful until Sir Mark nominated his son as the Tory candidate. The butler refused to second him after a row with his boss and in a fit of pique revealed his own intention to stand, whereupon Sir Mark refused to second him.

We were approaching the perfect by-election with no votes, voters or candidates when everyone seconded everyone else and the result was:

> Mark Wood, junior (Tory) (absent)   1
> Jennings (Whig)   0

It was the only election ever held at this promising constituency. Gatting was disenfranchised in 1832. The loss to British politics is incalculable.

THE LEAST SUCCESSFUL FOOTBALL TRAINER

In the first-ever World Cup the trainer of the American soccer team set an example which no other has yet managed to equal. In the 1930 semi-final Argentina had just scored a disputed goal against the USA. Shouting abuse at the referee as he travelled, our fellow dashed out to tend an injured player.

The 80,000 crowd roared with approval as he ran on to the pitch, threw down his medical bag, broke a bottle of chloroform and anaesthetized himself. He was carried off by his own team.

THE PUNCH THAT COUNTED

Given the choice between boxing and having a good time, the great Irish fighter Jack Doyle naturally chose the latter. Having won a few bouts and been hailed as the next heavyweight champion, he did not see the need for any more training, or even fighting.

In October 1938, however, after a seventeen-month lay-off, during which he attended a large number of parties, Doyle announced that he was returning to fight Eddie Phillips and this time he would be taking it seriously.

First, he arrived half an hour late, having been held up in a traffic jam outside Harringay Arena. In the second round he swung such a mighty punch that, when Phillips stepped sideways, Doyle knocked himself out, plunged through the ropes and landed next to the time keeper who solemnly counted to ten. Doyle then turned crooner and toured the music-halls as an attraction.

LEAST SUCCESSFUL EXPERIMENT
(INVOLVING A BAT)

Charles Waterton, the great Victorian traveller, devoted many years to the study of Vampire bats. For reasons of scientific thoroughness he felt that his research would not be complete until he had been attacked by one. To this end he arranged to sleep with just such a bat in his bedroom, while allowing his big toe to peep forth from the hammock.

After many weeks engaged in this venture Waterton remained woefully unbitten, unlike his Indian servant, Richard, who was nightly ravaged until he became too weak to perform his duties. 'His toe,' Waterton later complained bitterly, 'held all the attractions.'

THE LEAST SUCCESSFUL EXPERIMENT
(NOT INVOLVING A BAT)

A pioneering French inventor called Sauvant claimed in 1932 that he had perfected the world's first crash-proof aeroplane. From all accidents, he said, the aircraft and passengers would emerge completely unscathed.

On three occasions gendarmes removed the wheels from this contraption to prevent Monsieur Sauvant taking off in something that looked like a metallic boiled egg with prongs.

The irate inventor said it was perfectly safe and based upon his own experiments showing that if a hen's egg is placed inside an ostrich egg the chicken embryo would be unaffected by the experience. As one French paper said: 'No explanation of how the smaller egg is placed inside the larger one has yet appeared, nor have we been told what fate befalls the ostrich.'

Eventually, Monsieur Sauvant persuaded several friends to push him off an eighty-foot cliff in Nice. Confident that they would see him step out triumphantly waving, they peered down at the beach to see a total wreckage shattered beyond all hope of reconstruction and an inventor too dazed to leave his vehicle without the assistance of ropes and a team of enthusiastic admirers.

Later, when he had recovered, he declared that he was delighted with the success of the experiment.

THE WORST GOALKEEPER

In these days of defensive play it is the general cry that not enough goals are scored. No one has done more to change this situation than Chris Smith, the outstanding goalkeeper of Worthing Boys' Club in 1983.

In only eighteen matches this entertaining player let through 647 goals, an average of 35.9 per game. There were, of course, some days, when he did much better than this (he once let in nearer fifty, five of them in seven minutes). 'I don't always see the ball,' he said. 'It goes through my legs.'

Alarmingly, he was sent on a special training course, but his natural gifts could not be tampered with.

If there had been a net on the goalposts and he had not been forced to walk miles picking the ball up each time there is no telling what this fine boy might have achieved.

LEAST SUCCESSFUL ATTEMPT TO TRANQUILIZE AN ANIMAL

Mr Donald Kelly made his contribution to the art of tranquilization at Salem, Vancouver, in July 1980. While he was attempting to sedate an over-exuberant donkey, the syringe filled with Rompun, a horse tranquilizer, slipped.

He put out his hand to catch it, but the needle went into his ring finger. During the sleep which followed, Mr Kelly, an animal control officer, was described as 'looking very peaceful'. The donkey continued with its plans for the rest of the evening.

THE WORST BATSMAN

Although Patrick Moore, the astronomer, has had some success as a bowler, thanks to his 'medium-paced leg-breaks with a long, leaping, kangaroo-type action', we are prepared to overlook this in view of his outstanding contribution to the art of batting.

In a playing career which extends over half a century with the Lord's Taverners and his village team in Sussex, he has achieved a superb batting average of 0.8 runs an innings and has only broken into double figures once since 1949.

In his best season (1948) he scored only one run and that was from a dropped catch. That year he shattered the existing record for the most consecutive ducks (a measly eight) when he powered to a magnificent eighteen on the trot.

There are two possible explanations for his prowess. Mr Moore himself puts it down to having only two strokes, 'a cow shot to leg' and 'a desperate forward swat' which he uses in strict rotation. Furthermore, he does not wear spectacles when batting. 'Someone said it wouldn't make any difference if I wore binoculars.'

THE WORST DRIVER (FEMALE)

Few motorists have shown quite so much natural confidence on the road as Miss Bessie Cash who graced Oldham with her skills until 1982 when she voluntarily handed in her driving licence for her own safety.

After forty years with a clean motoring record, Miss Cash, who was seventy-nine, suddenly pulled that extra something out of the bag. Although travelling a customary route to her home address in Orange Avenue, she suddenly took the wrong turning and went down a cul-de-sac, onto the pavement, past thirteen shop-fronts, down a subway, through a labyrinth of tunnels, up into a shopping precinct, down another subway, in and out of some trees, narrowly missing forty-three shoppers and Miss Eunice Gerrard, a traffic warden, up onto another pavement, in and out of some more trees and straight at a policeman who tried to stop her, but had to jump out of the way and then watched her drive past a 'No entry' sign and right into a panda car. This brought her to the road she had been looking for.

Of her driving, Miss Gerrard, the traffic warden, said: 'I saw a green mini going down the subway. I thought. "No, it can't be." I ended up chasing it in and out of the trees.'

Explaining the incident, Miss Cash said afterwards: 'I just lost my way.' Realizing that she could not improve upon this performance, she handed in her licence and has not driven again.

THE LEAST CHARISMATIC POLITICIAN

In one of the outstanding political campaigns of the present century Mrs Beryl Shakes announced that she would be standing for parliament on condition that she didn't have to speak in public, attend meetings, talk to journalists or visit the constituency. 'Beryl's a shy person and she hasn't done anything like this before,' Mrs Mary Sanders, her party agent, said.

When selected as the Democratic Party candidate for Napier at Hawkes Bay in the 1987 New Zealand general elections, Mrs Shakes said: 'I won't go to Hawkes Bay. I want to stay at home and support my husband.' (Mr Graham Shakes was standing as the Democratic candidate for Wairarapa.)

A local newspaper profile of this exciting candidate said that she 'was educated at Wellington Technical College and took up sewing before her marriage'. She is also 'a keen gardener and a member of the Wairarapa branch of the New Zealand Soil Association'.

According to Norm Daken, who covered the campaign for the local *Hawkes Bay Herald Tribune*: 'We believe Mrs Shakes did visit the constituency for one day as part of her campaign, but we were not told of that event and had no opportunity to see her.'

When the votes were counted, she polled a magnificent 534, while her husband, who had campaigned enthusiastically throughout, got 27 amidst cries of 'Good one Graham'.

THE LEAST APPROPRIATE SPEECH

There have been few more fearless exponents of free speech than Baroness Trumpington of Sandwich. On 14 July 1986 she gave a powerful address to the House of Lords on the subject of 'expenses paid to child minders'.

'There has been much confusion on this matter,' she declaimed, her splendid sentiments resounding across that ancient chamber.

Their lordships listened in respectful silence as she called for a sane and sensible approach.

She had spoken for five minutes when this free-ranging diatribe built to an impressive climax. 'My lords,' she said, 'I have been speaking on the wrong subject.'

The debate was, in fact, on an amendment to the Social Security Bill. Tragically, she could have spoken for much longer, as not all of their lordships had noticed. Giving away a trick of the trade, the baroness said that she had brought the wrong notes.

THE FASTEST OWN GOAL

In an electric start to their match on 3 January 1977, Torquay United set an example that no other league side has equalled. Cambridge United kicked off and Ian Seddon struck a high ball down the length of the pitch, whereupon the brilliant Torquay centre-half, Pat Kruse, leaped above his own defence with lightning reactions. He headed the ball into his own net after only six seconds, scoring the fastest own goal in the history of league football.

A lesser team would have settled for that, but Torquay were on top form. In the forty-fourth minute they increased Cambridge's lead when their full back, Phil Sandercock, powered a spectacular header past his own goalkeeper, Tony Lee, who had been untroubled by Cambridge attacks.

In the second half Torquay slumped and drew level.

TEN

TEAMWORK MATTERS

In which Douglas S. Looney gets a scoop;
four freaks wow New York; and a tree
plays cricket.

THE LEAST SUCCESSFUL ANGLO-FRENCH FRIENDSHIP SOCIETY

Cross-channel confusion reached new heights in 1985 after the in-spired twinning of Godalming in Surrey with Joigny in France, two towns mainly noted for having nothing whatever in common.

Relations got off to a cracking start at the twinning ceremony. Perhaps wishing to show a Gallic side to his nature, the English president, Sir Richard Posnett, greeted the French visitors with a fine speech in which he said: 'I kiss all your women.' Unknown to him, the word *baiser* has acquired earthy four-letter overtones since his schooldays and the French were appalled to hear that Sir Richard was intending to fornicate with everybody.

Joigny wanted to send their many children on exchange schemes, but Godalming had an older population and could only muster nine infants. Instead they were keen to send over the Godalming amateur dramatic society to perform an evening of old-time music-hall. Over-whelming reluctance greeted this entire prospect in France, where a bicycle race round Godalming was suggested.

In Surrey this was felt likely to clog up the roads and so they proposed a swimming contest, but La Société de Natation de Joigny said the swimmers should meet for a banquet first, an idea the British resisted. The French then sent over the Joigny Chorale ('une trés, trés bonne chorale'). In Godalming they assumed it was a religious choir and booked the chapel at Charterhouse School only to find that it was 'a chaotic rock group who spent most of their time talking to each other between numbers'.

Things came to a head in 1987 when the Godalming Amateur Dramatics Society decided to hire a venue in Joigny and put on their old-time music-hall without waiting to be invited. The French accused 'Sir Posnett' of inflicting this entertainment upon them and they then resigned from the friendship circle *en masse* as a protest against the British.

In recognition of this great achievement Joigny was, that very week, awarded Le Drapeau d'Amitié Européen, the EEC's highest award for spreading European friendship.

LEAST SUCCESSFUL HISTORICAL RECONSTRUCTION

The Battle of Waterloo in 1815 began when the Highland Regiment marched through the town at 4 a.m. playing bagpipes.

When the Napoleonic Association attempted an accurate reconstruction in 1985 at the site of the original battle, the local Waterloo council would only allow one piper to play at 4 a.m., providing he marched through the back streets. Drowsy residents thought it was a cat being strangled.

Neither side camped on the battlefield: the French army stayed at a girls' school and the British were put up in a mental institution from which the inmates had been evicted for the weekend.

The Belgian participants were so obsessed with ceremonial marching that everyone was exhausted by the time the battle started. Then three Napoleons turned up which confused everyone. Furthermore, Wellington wasn't allowed to take his sword on the British Airways flight and so entered the fray unarmed. There was only one cannon and this had to leave half-way through the battle in order to arrive at Dunkirk in time for the ferry home. The British were outnumbered eight-to-one because everybody preferred the French uniforms and the final result was unclear.

When they finally got back onto British soil their only welcome was from HM Customs who confiscated the cannon for three hours.

THE HEAVIEST CRICKET DEFEAT

The most important team in the history of first-class cricket is the Dera Ismail Khan xi of Pakistan. Between 2 and 4 December 1964, they played an Ayub Trophy fixture at Lahore against a run-crazed Railways xi who batted until lunchtime on the third day. It was one dreary, predictable six after another for hours on end till they were all out for 851.

Out came Dera Ismail Khan in fine fettle. In no time the game was alive with thrills and excitement. Their first innings was a model of economy (they were all out for 32) and in the second innings they were all out for an even more thrilling 27 to achieve the heaviest defeat in the history of the game.

WORST RUGBY LEAGUE TEAM

The immense contribution of Doncaster to sporting life can never be overlooked. In 1975 it produced a rugby league team which was acknowledged as the worst professional sports side in the world. There can be no higher praise.

They have been bottom of the league more times than any other club and in 1977 they set a new all-comers record for the longest losing run of forty consecutive games. A television documentary was made recording the team's unquenchable spirit. It revealed that they do not recognize their own jerseys in muddy conditions and often tackle each other.

Their philosophical manager, Mr Tom Norton, said: 'When they lose I don't mind, so long as they entertain us. And, you know, it is possible to excite people even if you are getting thrashed.'

After a streaker had run topless across the field at Twickenham before an international match, Doncaster advertised in the local paper for a woman with a forty-two inch bust to do likewise at their own ground, Tatty's Field, in a last-ditch attempt to attract a crowd. 'We would quite happily settle for anything from thirty-eight inches upwards,' Mr Norton said when there was no immediate response.

In 1980 they became the first-ever club to put their whole team up for sale. Two days later their manager said: 'We haven't had any enquiries yet.'

THE WORST SOCCER TEAM

Thanks to the tremendous enthusiasm of boys, this is one of our most hotly contested categories. In 1972 the Norwich Nomads seemed to have it sewn up after a splendid season during which they lost all twenty of their games in the Norwich Boys League, scoring eleven goals and letting in 431 (an average of 21.55 goals let in per game).

Their mantle was taken over in the 1983 season by the Worthing Boys' Club under-twelve team which lost all eighteen of their games, scoring only six goals for with an impressive 647 against (an average of 35.9 goals let in per game). Widely hailed as the worst team in the country, they were given the annual Worthing award by the Mayor for generating national interest in the town. Five years later, they still had not won a game.

THE WORST-EVER BASEBALL TEAM

Formed in 1962, the New York Mets were given a tickertape welcome down Broadway before they had even touched a ball.

On 13 April the Department of Sanitation band struck up 'Hey, Look Me Over' and 40,000 spectators lined the route as the uniformed players rode past like conquering heroes in a rainbow-coloured procession of fourteen convertibles. Along the route 10,000 mock baseballs and bats were thrown into the crowd.

After this triumphant start they really got cracking and by 22 April they had equalled the Brooklyn Dodgers' 1918 record of losing nine games in a row. And by the end of this great debut they had lost more matches in one season than anyone else in the history of the game. The final figure was an impressive one hundred and twenty defeats.

THE LEAST ENTHUSIASTIC SOCCER TEAM

Blackburn Rovers showed definite sporting reluctance in their game against Burnley in 1891. In almost perfect conditions (it had been snowing steadily for three hours before kick-off and few fans bothered to turn up) Blackburn let in goals every quarter of an hour and were three-nil down at half-time.

When the interval went on an unusually long time, it became clear that Blackburn Rovers did not want to come out at all. Eventually, their team straggled on to the pitch, but the crowd could not help noticing that there were only seven of them.

Ten minutes later, Lofthouse of Blackburn had smacked the face of the Burnley captain, who retaliated with a punch. Both players were sent off. Feeling that this was an extremely good idea, the entire Blackburn team decided to follow them with the exception of the goalkeeper, a Mr Arthur, who remained at his post.

The referee, Mr Clegg, waited a few moments in the hope that Blackburn Rovers might reappear. When they failed to do so, the game restarted with the entire Burnley team bearing down upon Arthur. Nichol scored, but the goalkeeper successfully claimed it was offside and the referee abandoned the match.

The Blackburn captain later explained that this was not a protest against Lofthouse being sent off. They simply wanted to join him and were quite happy for Burnley to have the two points.

THE HEAVIEST SOCCER DEFEAT

The public flock to soccer matches in the hope of seeing goals scored. Thanks to Bon Accord Football Club, Scottish fans saw the greatest match ever played in the British Isles.

This entertaining side from Aberdeen let in thirty-six spectacular goals during a cup tie against Arbroath on 19 September 1885. It was the largest number ever conceded in a professional game.

The Bon Accord defence played throughout with a wonderfully open style that thrilled the happy crowd. A mere ten goals down at the interval, they wasted much time keeping the ball in midfield. But in the second half they got into their stride and dominated the play with their unselfish passing of the ball. Soon they had let in fifteen goals.

After sixty minutes a Bon Accord player came close to marring the whole game with their only shot at goal. Fortunately, it was intercepted by Collie of Arbroath.

The whistle went shortly after the thirty-sixth goal and Bon Accord trooped off to become the talking point of all Scotland. In an admiring report the local paper said they 'never seemed dismayed by the turn of events'. And quite rightly so. As the editorial went on to observe: 'It was the most amusing game ever seen in Arbroath.'

THE WORST POLICE FORCE

So great was the fame of the Philadelphia police force that they are said to have inspired the Keystone Kops.

In the early years they were so wholly untouched by personal discipline that a law had to be passed in 1830 to prohibit sleeping on duty.

In 1840 uniforms were introduced after a group of rioting medical students refused to believe that Patrolman Bramble was a police officer. The arrival of the scruffy figure merely intensified the disorder.

For ten years the entire force refused to wear the uniform and one officer resigned on the spot because it was 'derogatory to my feelings as an American'. Even when the Mayor of Philadelphia started wearing a helmet around the house and to all public engagements they were not encouraged. They argued that wearing a big hat and a vast silver star merely made them visible to the criminal classes.

By 1850 they were wearing the uniforms to report for duty and to sign off, but returned home in between to change into something more congenial. None of the force worked on Sundays which naturally became the peak period for criminal activity. On one weekday in 1857 no less than 114 of them were off sick.

In the twentieth century they have lost none of their old touch. A report in 1987 shows that they still exhaust themselves by zooming from one mundane call to another with sirens blaring. Furthermore, during 'Operation Grandpop' when officers posed as derelicts in order to attract muggers, they arrested hundreds of innocent people, including an elderly shoeshine boy.

Naturally, the people of Philadelphia are delighted with their police force and a recent opinion poll showed that 92 per cent think they are 'dedicated, professional and doing an excellent job'.

THE WORST BASKETBALL TEAM

Friendsville Academy Foxes notched up 128 consecutive defeats between 1967 and 1973, a record unequalled in the history of baseketball. Their coach says he used to give them pep talks until he 'discovered it was making them nervous'.

In 1970 Phil Patterson was named as Foxville's outstanding player. When Douglas S. Looney from the *National Observer* pointed out that Patterson had not scored a single point, the coach replied: 'You don't think scoring is everything, do you?'

In his report he gives the following verbatim account of their conversation:

> Looney: Is there anything this team does well?
> Coach: Not really.
> Looney: Are you making any progress?
> Coach: I couldn't truthfully say that we are.
> Looney: Do you like coaching?
> Coach: I don't care that much for basketball.

Their greatest defeat was 71-0 and their closest was 2-0, a scoreline ensured by a Friendsville player putting the ball in their own basket.

In no time they were nationally famous. ('There hasn't been so much excitement since the Baptist church burnt down.') So celebrated did they become that their mascot's fox suit was stolen by souvenir hunters.

Prominent in their gym were signs saying 'Character not victory is the important thing' and 'Humble in victory, praiseworthy in defeat'. The scene of unrelieved praiseworthiness at Foxville was disturbed only by their sole remaining cheerleader, Miss Patti Walsh, who kept bouncing up and down, shouting unhelpful slogans concerning the onward march to victory.

THE LEAST EXCITING RUGBY MATCH

Colwyn Bay Rugby team travelled fifty miles across the mountains of Snowdonia in 1966 to play Portmadoc. However, it was worth the trouble because the game fully surpassed expectations.

The referee ran out on to the pitch with all thirty players who limbered up, jumped around, sprinted in small circles, touched their toes and generally flexed themselves for action. Only when the teams lined up for kick-off did anyone realize that they did not have a ball.

At this point the game was abandoned.

THE PERFECT MATCH

Keen to play their annual needle match with Nairobi Harlequins in 1974, the fifteen members of Mombasa Rugby Football Club flew 475 miles to Uganda. During the one-and-a-half-hour journey they passed the no less enthusiastic Harlequins team thirty thousand feet below who were travelling in a fleet of cars to Mombasa. Nine hundred and fifty miles later both teams rang to find out what had happened to the opposition.

WORST BEHAVED RUGBY MATCH

The game between Abingdon and Didcot on 5 January 1983 went straight into the record books when the referee, Police Sergeant Peter Richmond, sent both teams off with five minutes left to play.

He blew his whistle, pointed to the dressing-room, walked off muttering 'I've had enough of this', got into his car and drove away to write a blistering report to the Oxfordshire Rugby Union. It was the first time in the game's history that 100 per cent marching orders had been issued.

According to the players, there had been 'a bit of a scuffle'.

WORST BOWLING AVERAGE

Wisden Cricketers' Almanack credits Malcolm Nash as the bowler who has enabled the opposition to score most runs from a single over. Thanks to his work, Gary Sobers playing for Nottinghamshire notched up six consecutive sixes in the 1968 match against Glamorgan at Swansea.

The Times diary, however, has pointed to an even more rewarding bowler who graced a fixture in Western Australia during 1894. 'Cogg' by name, he ran in a slow, loping fashion towards the crease and lobbed a ball which the visiting batsman whacked off towards the boundary.

When it landed in the three-pronged fork of a nearby tree, the umpire ruled that the batsmen should keeping running as the ball was still visible.

Two fielders climbed up the tree, but the lower branches collapsed under their weight. Then they tried chopping the tree down and much time was spent in the fruitless search for an axe. Then they got hold of a rifle and the sleepy afternoon rang with a barrage of flying bullets.

By this time the visitors had completed 286 runs and declared.

They were now sitting in the pavilion appreciating the extravagant fielding of the home side.

THE LEAST DISCIPLINED SOCCER TEAMS

Competition here is intense. On 2 February 1975 the entire Glencraig United football team and their two substitutes were all booked before they had even left the dressing room. The referee, a Mr Tarbet of Bearsden, took exception to the chant which greeted his arrival.

In November 1969 all twenty-two players, including one who went to hospital, were booked in the match between Tongham Youth and Hawley, which one of the players later described as 'a good hard game'. Rising to his task, the referee, John McAdam, then booked a linesman for dissent. 'At one stage in the match he threw the flag on the floor and after that never seemed to have the same interest in the game.'

Some claim that this was the wildest game ever played, but such people were not present on 25 February 1951 when Lily Mills FC met the Ukrainian Sports Club, Rochdale, in the first round of the local charity cup. The referee not only ordered both teams off, but also cautioned the crowd who had joined in the mêlée.

THE WORST CRICKET TEAM

Formed in 1950 at University College, Oxford, the Utopers XI played for thirty-three years before conceding their first victory. Explaining their team's astonishing consistency, the college handbook said: 'It is not the winning, but the taking part that counts. Indeed, what alternative was there?'

The 1980 season got off at the usual cracking pace with well deserved defeats by Mansfield College, the London Utopers, New

College and the Captain Scott Invitation XI. They kept this standard up throughout their annual tour of Dorchester-on-Thames.

Then the unbelievable happened. According to the college magazine, 'The Utopers' spirit came in for a severe blow when they met the combined forces of the Southern Counties Open University, a team genuinely more dedicated to playing the game for the game's sake. For once victory could not be staved off despite gallant attempts from all concerned.'

Their nerve was broken and from that day the Utopers went on to a series of wins. So appalled were the older players that in 1988 the original team was planning to re-form in order to recapture their lost verve.

THE LEAST SUCCESSFUL BATON TWIRLING

Noted for the height, range and drama of their twirls, members of the Ventura Baton Twirling Troupe surprised even themselves on one occasion in the late 1960s.

During an Independence Day march past, one of their batons hit a power cable, blacked out the area, started a grass fire and put the local radio station off the air. 'They were on form,' the mayor said.

THE WORST-EVER VARIETY ACT

The worst act in the history of light entertainment was almost certainly the Cherry Sisters from Cedar Rapids, Iowa. Their performance was so entertaining that a wire net had to be erected across the footlights to protect them from the shower of potatoes, apples, cabbages and other tributes that were regularly hurled at this unique musical quartet. The sisters themselves insisted that it was the work of envious rivals.

Their act opened with Aggie, Effie, Lizzie and Jessie walking awk-

wardly to the centre of the stage in shapeless, flame-red gowns, hats and woollen mittens of their own making. Three of them were tall, thin and sang, while Jessie was short, fat and played a bass drum.

They stood there acknowledging the ecstatic hoots which greeted their arrival and then launched into a uniquely strained soprano version of 'Ta-ra-ra-boom-dee-ay' that included the verse

Cherries ripe, boom-dee-ay
Cherries red, boom-dee-ay
The Cherry Sisters
Have come to stay.

The song was accompanied by a range of hearty gestures that were refreshingly untarnished by female grace. There were also intermittent thumps upon the drum. The audience sat transfixed with disbelief until the Cherry Sisters shuffled off the stage, showing not the slightest trace of nervousness or of the talent normally associated with this line of work.

In 1896 they were taken to New York by Oscar Hammerstein, the impresario, who said, 'I have tried putting on the best acts and it hasn't worked. Now I'm trying the worst.'

The *New York Times* review of their opening night on 17 November was headed 'Four Freaks From Iowa'. In it the critic said that 'all too obviously they were genuine products of the barnyard and the kitchen ... never before did New Yorkers see anything in the least like the Cherry Sisters' and suggested that their performance might be due to poor diet.

Another critic wrote that 'a locksmith with a strong rasping file could earn ready wages taking the kinks out of Lizzie's voice'.

Their repertoire also included 'I'm Out Upon The Mash, Boys', 'Curfew Must Not Ring Tonight', 'Don't You Remember Sweet Alice, Ben Bolt' and 'The Modern Young Man', a recitation. With a growing reputation as the world's worst variety act, they constantly played to capacity crowds all over America.

Hammerstein's hunch paid off.

ELEVEN

THE CULTURAL EXPLOSION

In which earwigs are hailed in verse; Dr Livingstone is covered with grass; and actors go blue to avoid confusion.

MOST LINES FORGOTTEN BY ONE ACTOR

In one of the great stage performances of our time Mr Paul Greenwood breathed new life into a familiar old play by forgetting almost every line of his part at the Barbican Theatre, London, on 24 July 1984.

At the opening night of *The Happiest Days of Your Life* he single-handedly transformed an otherwise predictable show. The great actor strode confidently onto the stage and placed his golf bag on the table. It immediately slid off, signalling that we were in the presence of a master.

After saying a few lines correctly, perhaps to show what a dull evening it would be without his intervention, he began rummaging in his pockets so he could 'take a note' as the script demanded. It all began when his propelling pencil didn't have any lead and then his pen didn't have any ink and then he realized there was total silence on stage while he was supposed to be speaking.

Now elegantly flustered, his face was suffused with the finest expression of blankness ever seen on the London stage. He launched into a bravura selection of original lines that would have come as a great surprise to the playwright.

In Act Two he varied his performance and began saying everybody else's lines, whereupon he turned to the audience and said: 'I'm sorry, we'll have to stop because I'm talking nonsense up here. You see, there was no lead in my pencil.' When a colleague ad-libbed that 'this has always been your problem' it brought the house down.

By Act Three the excellent Mr Greenwood was completely liberated from the plot. 'Shall I start again?' he asked the enthralled audience. 'Yes,' they roared back, wishing to bask anew in such an original performance.

One theatre critic took this opportunity to review the prompter who was 'such a feature of the evening', while *The Times* hailed it as 'memory loss on a grand scale'.

THE WORST OPERA PROGRAMME NOTES

The Genoa Opera Company staged a memorable production of Bizet's *Carmen* in 1981. Even more memorable were the programme notes explaining the plot.

ACT ONE: Carmen, a cigarmakeress from a tobago factory loves Don Jose of the mounting guard. Carmen takes a flower from her corsets and lances it to Don Jose. (Duet: 'Talk me of my mother.') There was noise inside the tobago factory and revolting cigarmakeresses burst onto the stage. Carmen is arrested and Don Jose is ordered to mounting guard on her but she subduces him and lets her escape.

ACT TWO: The Tavern. Carmen sings (Aria: 'The sistrums tinkling.') Enter two smugglers ('Ho, we have in mind a business.') Enter Escamillio, a Balls fighter. Carmen refuses to penetrate because Don Jose has liberated her from prison. He just now arrives. (Aria: 'Slop here who comes.') But here are the bugles singing his retreat. Don Jose will leave and draws his sword. Called by Carmen's shrieks the two smugglers interfere with her. Jose is bound to dessert. Final Chorus: 'Opening Sky Wandering Life.'

ACT THREE: A rocky landscape. Smugglers chatter. Carmen sees her death in the cards. Don Jose makes a date with her for the next Balls fight.

ACT FOUR: A Place in Seville. Procession of Ball-fighters. The roaring of Balls is heared in the arena. Escamillio enters (Aria and chorus: Toreador. Toreador. All hail the Balls of a toreador.') Enter Don Jose (Aria: 'I besmooch you.') Carmen repels him. She wants to join with Escamillio now chaired by the crowd. Don Jose stabbs her. (Aria: 'Oh, rupture, rupture.') He sings: 'Oh, my subductive Carmen.'

THE WORST LAUREATE

At the end of the nineteenth century Joseph Gwyer set himself up as the unofficial Poet Laureate of Britain. Why, he reasoned, should the Queen have only one of these when he himself had ample free time from his work as a potato salesman in Penge to perform such literary services.

For this task he had three main qualifications. First, he had no access to state occasions of any kind. Second, it goes without saying that he was unblighted at birth by literary gifts. And, third, he had a rigorous poetic honesty so that if things were too hard for him to describe, he would quite simply say so.

At one procession featuring the Prince of Wales he wrote:

> At evening too the dazzled light
> Illumed (sic) the darkness of the night
> I can't paint it for reasons best.
> Twas grand, though I in crowd was pressed.

Over a period of 20 years he bombarded members of the royal family with his accounts of their doings, which elicited curt and frosty letters of acknowledgement from their private secretaries.

Undeterred by this coolness, Gwyer produced in 1875 a volume of his work, entitled *Poems (Commended by royalty)*, in which he included all of these frosty letters by way of recommendation. On the title-page he further announced that he could also send, on a sale-or-return basis, sacks of potatoes and, indeed, gilt-framed photographs of himself and his cart-horse.

This book includes his timeless lines upon the funeral of Dr Livingstone, which he did not actually attend:

> Heap on more grass was his request
> As hapless now he laid to rest

It also contains an 'Ode on the Visit of the Shah of Persia', which is largely devoted to his teetotal enthusiasm:

> Intoxicating draughts he never does drink

THE CULTURAL EXPLOSION

If this we copied should we not be better, think?

When reviewing his collected works, the *New York Tribune* said that young people wavering between Mr Gwyer's poetry and his potatoes should unhesitatingly choose the latter.

THE LEAST SUCCESSFUL JUDGES

An esteemed panel gathered in February 1987 to judge 387 entries in the New York Chair Fair.

After some rarified discussion at the New International Design Centre they awarded the prize for the best Ad Hoc Avant-garde Chair to Mr Tom Musorafita. The name was not known to any of the distinguished audience.

Only when the prize was awarded did they learn that he was a construction worker on the as yet unfinished New Design Centre. When he saw the entries arriving, he decided to make a seat from the leftovers in his skip as a joke.

Looking at the nailed up combination of a cardboard drum, a piece of plasterboard and a green plastic lid, the award-winning craftsman said: 'I can't believe this piece of garbage won anything. I had to look up "ad hoc" to make sure they weren't yanking me around.'

In praise of the judges' adventurous choice, a critic from *Design Week* magazine said: 'It was actually quite comfortable because there was a bit of give in the cardboard drum.'

THE WORST ORCHESTRAL TOUR

In August 1977 the London Sinfonietta visited Tunisia to give two concerts at the Tabarka and Carthage Music Festival.

On landing at Tunis Airport they found that the courier, who

was to transfer them by bus to Tabarka, was not there, nor was the bus. Eventually, the courier did turn up but there was still no sign of the bus and it was two hours before they embarked upon a hair-raising journey to the Mimosas Hotel, where 20 rooms were reserved. On arrival the hotel had, naturally, never heard of them nor of the Carthage and Tabarka Music Festival.

The orchestra spent the night on the beach without bedclothes, pillows, food or drink in huts belonging to a disused Club Méditerranée. Coincidentally, Mr Michael Vyner, the orchestra's artistic director, dreamed of his mother advising him to become a lawyer and to avoid the world of professional music.

Next day, no one in Tabarka knew anything about a concert that night or any other and the Carthage end of the festival 'seemed not to care one way or the other what was happening in their sister town'. The orchestra abandoned the first concert, played the second and returned to Heathrow Airport with a deep sense of gratitude.

THE DUD BOOK FAIR

A record number of visitors poured into the 1982 York Book Fair, probably because its central feature was the first 'Dud Books of All Times' exhibition. Never before had such a powerful collection of completely unsaleable volumes been gathered together under one roof.

The imposing entrance to the Assembly Rooms was specially decked out for the occasion with vivid wallpaper, fairy lights and a dayglo pink signboard.

The most popular book on show was *The List of Stop Cocks in the Liver Building, Liverpool 1912*. This was closely followed by a signed copy of *The Philosophy of Elbert Hubbard*.

Even before the exhibition opened, one natural history expert snapped up copies of both *The Common Teasel as a Carnivorous Plant* and *Ostrich Egg-Shell Cups of Mesopotamia in Ancient and Modern Times*.

The early history of sanitation was fully represented by such work as *The Law Relating to Sewers and Drains 1904*, while the travel section included *Uganda For A Holiday* by Sir Frederick Treves and *The Little I Saw of Cuba* by Burr McIntosh.

In the biography and memoir department *The Mother of Goethe* made a happy companion to *I was Hitler's Aunt*. *Heroes and Heroines of Libya* was a huge hit, as was *Jokes Cracked by Lord Aberdeen* in a tartan cover. The only disappointment was that the promised copy of *The Romance of Leprosy* by E. Mackerchar did not materialize.

THE CRITIC WHO REVIEWED THE WRONG SHOW

How necessary is it for a critic to see the production that he is reviewing? Opinions differ on this, but Heuwell Tircuit of the *San Francisco Chronicle* has done much to further the view that such details only clutter the mind.

In August 1987 this great critic wrote a devastating attack on the San Francisco Ballet's performance of the *pas de deux* from Bizet's opera *La Jolie Fille de Perth*.

In a stimulating tirade, headed 'San Francisco Ballet Misses a Step', Tircuit hit top gear. 'Either the San Francisco Ballet is being overworked or under-rehearsed,' he roared. For a start, he was not impressed by the dancers who 'looked a tad dumpy'. He found that David McNaughton was 'not up to his best'. And, as for Ludmilla Lopukhova, 'her potato-drenched Russian training seemed less heavy than in the past. But she, when added to Tomasson's dank choreography, didn't quite come through'.

Perhaps this was because the performance was cancelled that night and replaced by *Ballet For Five Male Dancers* in which Miss Lopukhova naturally did not appear.

In his report Mr Tircuit estimated that there were 10,000 people in the audience at the open-air theatre. His newspaper later estimated that he had not been one of them. Defending his imaginative review, he said that he attended the performance, but felt so ill that he was unaware of what he was watching.

THE WORST OPENING SENTENCE OF A NOVEL

No one has done more to encourage our sort of novelist than Professor Scott Rice of the San Jose State University. In 1983 he launched the Bulwer-Lytton contest for the worst opening sentence to a novel and was instantly flooded with 10,000 entries from fifty countries.

He started the contest 'to fill a need'. Most literary contests, he said, are inherently unfair, favouring as they do talent, sensibility and intelligence. 'They are callously neglectful of the mediocre masses, those who might be authors if they had any craft, vision or message.'

The contest was named after the nineteenth-century British novelist, Edward Bulwer-Lytton, in whose work a glass of beer is always 'a nectarian beverage' and a bedroom is 'somnambular accommodation' and a man lighting his pipe is described as 'applying the Promethean spark to his tube'.

Just a few examples show the high standard of entrant in this now annual event. Some are domestic dramas:

> 'The variety of quirks, ailments and miscellaneous disfigurements that can strike the average supermarket cart is truly amazing,' she said.

Others set a mood:

> It was autumn, and the fog clung to the old house as it did nearly every autumn (with the exception of the previous year, which had been incredibly sunny) like damp gauze on a soldier's wound, except there was no blood, as he stopped the car at the kerb and gazed thoughtfully towards the house.

Yet others launch into the ever-popular spy genre:

> It came to him in a cocaine rush as he took the Langley exit that if Aldrich had told Filipov about Hancock only Tulfgengian could have known that the photograph which Wagner had shown to Maximov on the jolting S-bann was not the

photograph of Kessler that Bradford had found at the dark, sinister house in the Schillerstrasse the day that Straub told Percival that the man on the bridge had not been Aksakov but Pawstovsky, which meant that it was not Kleist but Kruger that Cherensky had met in the bleak, wintry Grunewald and that, therefore, only Frau Epp could have known that Muller had followed Droysen to the steamy aromatic cafe in the Beethovenstrasse where he told Buerger that Todorov had known since the Liebermann affair that McIntyre had not met Stoltz at the Golitzer Bahnhof but instead had met Sommer in the cavernous Anhalter Bahnhof.

Anyone wishing to study the entries in more detail is recommended to read *It Was A Dark And Stormy Night* published by Sphere Books in 1986, the uplifting volume in which Professor Rice reprints the whole lot.

THE WORST-EVER NOVELIST

In the 1940s ardent admirers claimed that Mrs Amanda McKittrick Ros was the worst novelist in the English or any other language. Nothing has happened since to alter this happy state of affairs. Born in 1861, Amanda Malvina Fitzalan Anna Margaret McLelland McKittrick Ros was also manager of the local lime kiln.

Blessed with the gift of alluring alliteration, this Belfast housewife wrote four novels: *Delina Delaney, Irene Iddesleigh, Donald Dudley* and *Helen Huddleson* (in which Lord Raspberry pays unwanted attentions to a country girl). On a typical day, characters like Rodney Rupert, Oscar Otwell and Marjorie Mason feel able to say, 'Leave me now deceptive demon of deluded mockery. Lurk no more around the vale of vanity, like a vindictive viper.'

Her style was full of such burning intensity that mere sense was rarely allowed to interfere with it. Her characters never sit in a room, they are 'sharing its midst'; nothing is ever white — female hands, passing clouds and certain tablecloths are always 'snowy';

and troublesome women are 'most retorting'. Trousers, meanwhile, are 'the southern necessity'. She is also extremely fond of the word 'mushroom' which appears more often than is strictly required.

Transcending conventional grammar, she often began with a phrase that properly belonged to the previous sentence. The following is a typical example:

> Her uncle replied 'Ah dear Helen, I feel heart sick of this frivolous frittery fraternity of fragiles flitting round and about Earth's huge plane wearing their mourning livery of religion as a cloak of design tainted with the milk of mockery,' wiping his moistened brow with a crimson handkerchief, while Helen acquiesced, Henry Jnr remaining silent.

She was a stout woman given to black hair-nets, who had the words 'At home always to the honourable' printed on her calling cards. Rightly convinced of her own genius, she condemned all critics of her work as donkeyosities, egotistical earthworms, hog-washing hooligans, critic cads, random hacks of illiteration, talent wipers of wormy order, the gas-bag section, poking hounds, poisonous apes, maggotty numbskulls, evil-minded snapshots of spleen and, worst of all, the mushroom class of idiotics.

Although her novels were unforgivably out of print soon after publication, she said: 'I feel I am a great favourite as a writer. I will be talked about at the end of a thousand years. I afford pleasure and give satisfaction to the million and one who continually thirst for aught from my pen. I also know I write different from any known writer or organizer of prose.' She also wrote poetry (See Worst Poet).

THE WORST POET

Having exhausted the possibilities of the novel, Amanda McKittrick Ros turned her talents to the poetic field. She produced two volumes, entitled *Poems of Puncture* and *Fumes of Formation*.

The remarkable thing about her poetry was its range. She could write religious verse, as in her 'Ode To Easter':

Dear Lord, the day of eggs is here.

And in 'The Engineer Divine' she discusses the possibility of an electrified railway line to heaven:

> The current of faith from the battery of prayer
> Can act on the magnet of love.
> With movements produced by a Motor Divine
> Which matchless perfection displays,
> The engine of Truth as it runs up the line
> The Train of Salvation conveys.

As a war poet, she had similar conviction:

> We know you'll do your duty and come to little harm
> And if you meet the Kaiser, cut off his other arm.

Her descriptive verse was also able to capture the spirit of a place, as in her reflective lines upon Poets' Corner at Westminster Abbey:

> Holy Moses! Take a look!
> Flesh decayed in every nook,
> Some rare bits of brain lie here,
> Mortal loads of beef and beer.

When in more savage mood, she launched vitriolic attacks upon lawyers. She wrote an entire poem, for example, denouncing Mickey 'Monkeyface' McBlear, a local solicitor who had the audacity to represent her opponents in a lawsuit.

Above all, Mrs Ros was a moralist. In her poem 'I love to see a lady nice and natural at any price' she inveighs against the modern woman who behaves like a man:

> And smoke and spit, no matter where,
> And very often curse and swear,
> I lose my temper o'er these arts
> That stamp such women – Dirty Clarts.

THE LEAST SUCCESSFUL FEMINIST BOOK

Virago books launched in 1987 a new series of feminist books for teenagers. In the first batch was *Down The Road, Worlds Away* by Ranila Khan, whom the publishers described as 'an unknown Islamic authoress'. It was a sensitive collection of short stories showing the problems that Asian girls face growing up in an oppressive, male-dominated society.

The book was withdrawn soon after publication when Virago discovered that it was, in fact, written by an unknown Anglican vicar called the Reverend Toby Forward, who afterwards explained that he 'did it because people often don't take Anglican vicars all that seriously'.

LEAST SUCCESSFUL FRINGE SHOW

The Edinburgh Festival fringe was set alight in 1983 by an outstanding production of *Ubu Roi* that closed after only fifteen minutes of its first and last performance.

Advance publicity whetted the appetite for 'the first appearance in Britain by an extraordinary West Berlin ensemble (Freie Theateranstalt) with a pig, cockatoos and several parrots who create a visual symphony and a threatening stillness'.

The leading actor and director Hermann van Harten said the production did not have the animals as advertised because no one told him they would have to be put into quarantine. The parrots and cockatoos were dispensable, but the pig was essential because it played the role of Ubu Roi's wife. At the last minute they had borrowed a pig called Rust from the local East Lothian city farm and the play's opening was delayed for five days due to intensive pig training.

On the big night Rust just 'oinked around the place', refusing to jump up and down as the part required.

After only a quarter of an hour on the opening night van Harten passed out on stage with exhaustion. A member of the cast then stepped forward to say that the show was so awful they had decided to scrap it and give everyone their money back.

THE UNLUCKIEST STAGE SHOW

Knowing how superstitious theatre people are, Mr Lawrence Wright announced that his thirteenth production at the North Pier, Blackpool, was in fact his fourteenth. The fates now thwarted, he opened *On With The Show* in the summer of 1938.

First, the theatre burned down and all the props were destroyed. After that things began to go seriously wrong. The show was transferred to the smaller pavilion, where Tessie O'Shea slipped, sprained her wrist and was unable to play her ukulele. Then Harry, of The Five Sherry Brothers, was rushed off with gastric troubles, an ailment also caught by the novelty vocalist, Peggy Desmond, who was out of action for a week.

Robert Naylor lost his voice, while Frank Randle had to have all his teeth pulled out and stood there in his gums for the rest of the run. Dorrane of 'Alexis and Dorrane Speciality Dancers' was ordered to take a complete rest, two menbers of the Health and Beauty Chorus sprained ankles and one of the high-speed dancing Viennese Romancers fell upstairs and hurt her leg. Mr W. M. Morris, the manager, collapsed and the wardrobe mistress, Mrs E. Perry, fell and sprained her arm.

It was then discovered that there were 13 people in the cast, 13 musicians in the band and 13 songs in the show.

THE WORST PERFORMANCE

In 1978 the South Australian Arts Council arranged for a touring theatre company to visit the remote town of Barmera with a play called *A Bard's Banquet*. A special feature of this production was that the Elizabethan banquet taking place on stage would also be shared by the audience who would eat and drink throughout the show.

On 7 August 280 guests arrived at the Bonny Theatre where the courses were carefully timed to coincide with the acts of the play. By 9 p.m. there was still no sign of the lorry which was making a 240-kilometre journey from Adelaide with pre-heated food.

The curtain went up two hours late and the man who had arranged everything went on stage to apologize for the delay. He announced that the actors had agreed to mime the banquet and then retreated, having been hit in the neck by a tomato. It was the only food that anyone had seen all night. Instead the audience had become seriously lubricated.

According to Mr J. Maxwell, the Arts Council touring manager, the famished audience was 'rowdy, unruly and beyond caring for the finer parts of drama'. Soup was hurriedly rustled up in the kitchen, but this only gave the audience something to throw.

This fabulous evening came to a crescendo when the cast left the stage complaining that no less than two couples were making love in the audience and that this was proving a greater draw than anything they were able to do.

At 11 p.m. the lorry driver walked in saying that he had achieved three flat tyres and turned the lorry over once. When the food finally arrived, it was promptly thrown at the cast as they left the stage.

THE MUSICAL THAT NOBODY UNDERSTOOD

After a career packed with theatrical triumphs Sir Peter Hall, the British director, put on *Via Galactica* and showed that when he really tries he can produce something in an altogether different class. He cannot, however, claim credit for the sci-fi musical's plot, which was so complex that the Uris Theatre in New York inserted a special explanatory sheet in the programme.

It explains how all the people in the musical are painted blue 'to avoid wars and confusion' and wear cone-shaped spinning hats to control their emotions. The story was based on the life and times of a space-age sanitation expert.

The *New York Times* drama critic, Clive Barnes, wrote: 'The well-publicized use of trampolines, to suggest weightlessness, suggests nothing more than people pointlessly bouncing up and down on trampolines.' The mechanical space garbage cart floating in the sky was 'all too clearly chained to the stage' and the spaceship from Earth 'looks like a displaced light fitting'.

The show closed after seven performances.

THE WORST WEST END PLAY

At the age of eighty-three the Reverend Walter Reynolds wrote *Young England*, a play which received such wonderfully bad reviews that it played to full houses for 278 performances at the Victoria Palace before transferring by public demand to two other theatres in the West End of London.

Intended by its author as a serious work celebrating the triumph of good over evil and the virtues of the Boy Scout Movement, it was received as an uproarious comedy.

Before long, audiences had learned the key lines and were joining in at all the choicest moments. The scoutmistress rarely said the line 'I must go and attend to my girls' water' without at least fifty voices in good-humoured support.

The plot, which was never cheapened by a sense of humour, tells of Major Carlingford, a betrayer of women, shady promoter and sanctimonious humbug, who spends the greater part of the evening conspiring with his scoundrel son to ruin a popular and heroic young man who is not only a scoutmaster, a town councillor and a parliamentary candidate, but also a talented engineer destined to improve the appearance of the River Thames at Charing Cross.

When the play opened in September 1934 at the Victoria Palace Theatre the *Daily Telegraph's* critic wrote: 'The villain makes plain his villainy by constantly wearing a top hat in the depths of the country. His son, "the second robber", is some sort of officer in the Boy Scouts and brings shame upon that highly respected body by committing his major crime while dressed in his uniform. But he at least has the grace to get into immaculate evening dress proper to his kind when he wants to get drunk.'

The show went from strength to strength, even though its clergyman author periodically roamed the aisles remonstrating with hecklers and shaking his fists.

THE WORST POEM EVER WRITTEN

Although this is a highly subjective matter, there is a strong case for arguing that Mr Theophile Marzials' poem, 'A Tragedy', written in 1837, has never been surpassed.

The Pre-Raphaelite poet had honey-blond hair and caused a stir by saying in a loud voice 'Am I not the darling of the British Museum Reading Room?' while seated in that very establishment. He once recited this poem in his deep baritone voice at a soirée organized by Dante Gabriel Rossetti, the poet and painter. In the thoughtful silence which followed Rossetti said it was 'written on a plan absolutely inadmissable'.

The opening stanza establishes the elegiac mood of the poem:

> Death!
> Plop.
> The barges down in the river flop.
> Flop, plop,

After a page or so in this exciting vein Marzials really gets going:

> To the oozy waters that lounge and flop
> On the black scrag-piles, where the loose cords plop,
> As the raw wind whines in the thin tree-top.
> Plop, plop.

Before long he is in top gear:

> At the water that oozes up, plop and plop,
> On the barges that flop
>   And dizzy me dead.
> I might reel and drop.
>   Plop
>   Dead.

With a tactful reticence that is rare nowadays he does not tell us exactly what his problem is until two-thirds of the way through this lengthy poem. Eventually, it transpires that somebody has gone off with somebody else's fiancée (whose is not clear). However, the fact is recorded in a rising tide of emotion that takes us to the poem's unforgettable conclusion:

> Ugh: and I knew!
>   Ugh!
> So what do I care,
> And my head is as empty as air –
>   I can do,
>   I can dare
>   (Plop, plop,
>   The barges flop
>   Drip, drop.)
>   I can dare, I can dare!
> And let myself all run away with my head,
> And stop.
>   Drop
>   Dead.
>   Flip, flop.
>   Plop.

Many have puzzled away at the exact meaning of the lines:

> And let myself all run away with my head,
> And stop.

But scholars of all nations agree it was a masterpiece.

THE LEAST INFORMATIVE BOOK

During 1944 Mr Keith Odo Newman wrote a book entitled *250 Times I Saw A Play*. It is an account of his visits to every performance of the same stage show, including matinées. The charm of the book lies in the fact that, while he wishes to give us a complete understanding of this experience, he nowhere tells us what the play was, who wrote it, where it was performed or who acted in it.

Describing his feat as 'sequential attendance', he argued that this would give him 'heightened sensitivity' to this play and to the nature of all drama. What it actually did was drive him nuts.

The book is packed full of insights. At one point he observes that 'the longer I continued my attendance, the more did I become convinced that for a play to be fully appreciated and enjoyed it must not only be played, but played before an audience'.

Although he proudly announces that he himself thought up the title of the play, he still cannot be tempted to share it with us. Instead, he moves on to a chapter headed 'Audience and Actor' in which he develops his extensive views on sado-masochism. 'It may well be asked by the reader how this discourse about sadism and masochism is relevant to the study. I believe it is,' he writes. Happily, he does not attempt to say why, but restricts himself to giving us a potted biography of the Marquis de Sade.

In the chapter on 'Impersonation' he considers at some length the difference between acting and impersonating. The next chapter is entitled 'Back To The Play', but rather cleverly he does not go back to the play at all. Instead he continues with his views on impersonation. The book ends with his guess that the mental age of the audience was around sixteen.

Asked for his comments, George Bernard Shaw replied: 'I don't know what to say about this book', a tribute that was cheerfully printed on the cover.

THE LEAST CONVINCING STAGE CORPSE

Any actor can bring a character to life on stage. Only the really talented can keep one alive long after the playwright's directions insist that he is dead.

On 30 July 1987 the audience of the Olympia Theatre, Dublin, were enthralled by Patrick Mower's performance as Clifford, the brilliant young thing, in Ira Levin's play 'Death Trap'. According to the script of this thriller, he is supposed to be killed with a crossbow in the penultimate scene before the policeman and the clairvoyant come on.

On the great night, however, the crossbow was too tight to load and the evening before it had been too loose. Infuriated by this faulty prop, Mr Mower made the play even more thrilling by appearing on stage when he was supposed to be dead and then haranguing the stage management team.

Bringing Clifford back to life in this way made a fine, dramatic ending and corrected the playwright's error in depriving everyone of this pleasing character so soon.

THE WORST LINE OF VERSE CONTROVERSY

Competition is intense and controversy will always rage as to the worst line of verse ever written. Any debate must always take into account the work of the Victorian clergyman, Edward Dalton, who in 1875 was inspired by the power of steam trains to write:

> The steam escapes in hissing tide,
> Crunch, crunch, thud, rud, dubber-dub-dub,
> Thudder, rubber, dub-dub, dub-a-rub-rub-rub.

Leaving nothing to chance the poem ends several pages later:

> Crash! Crash! What's that? A peal of thunder?

A rattling volley? No, a bridge, a bridge we've just passed under.

Edward Newman, by contrast, is obsessessed in 1855 with insects. His detailed epic of the creepie-crawlie world begins:

> First of walkers come the earwigs,
> Earwigs or FORNFICULINA.

In the field of religious verse the Reverend A. Freston wrote in 1787:

> Creation be! And lo! Creation was!

which makes it sound much easier than one feels sure was the case.

Stephen Fawcett (1872) was both a romantic poet and a curious one:

> What has he whispered in beauty's lug?

While Edward Caswell during 1858 stood in healthy awe of the natural world:

> Ye Heat and Cold!
> Creatures most opposite!
> Betwixt you twain oft times
> In a strange doubt I stand,
> Which out of which proceeds;
> Nor what ye are, nor whence,
> Can I at all divine . . .

As one critic has observed: 'After this initial confession of ignorance, one would expect the poet to mug up the subject a little before proceeding further, but not a bit of it: he gives us another 61 lines.'

William Igglesden asks a perfectly reasonable question in 1858:

> Antarctic wanderer, whither art thou roaming?

While Israel Thomas Jacob is more of a regional poet:

> Deeply grieved in Wales were thousands
> When they heard of Irving's death

John Stanyan Bigg, the editor of the *Ulverston Advertiser*, writes in a more tragic vein:

> Hush! Place thy hand upon my burning brow,
> And I will tell thee what has happ'd and now

It transpires that one thing after another happened to his unfortunate family:

> And three lie in their gore
> Down by the great hall door
> And Fred and I are all that are alive.

And all poets appeal to the muse for inspiration and none with a more direct honesty than Pownoll Toker Williams in 1889:

> Please tell me what to say and
>   how to say it;
> I'm going to try to and sing
>   the Lake at Aix

THE MOST REJECTION SLIPS

John Creasey made an important contribution to world literature over a period of seven years. He showed early promise when his first thriller, *The Men Who Died Laughing*, came back from the publishers almost immediately. Three months later he completed a school novel, *Our Glorious Term*, and this proved even less popular. His third book, *The Captain of the Fifth*, was completely unacceptable as were *The Mysterious Mr Rocco*, *Mystery at Mamby House* and *The Flying Turk*.

With the return of *Dazzle and the Red Bombers* the great man of letters was getting into his stride.

By 1925 he had received 743 rejection slips before getting his first book published and losing all interest for us. One possible reason for his achievement is that he once claimed to have written two of these books in a week and still spent half a day playing cricket.

THE LEAST SOLEMN MASS

Beethoven's *Missa Solemnis* was given its most dramatic performance ever at Acton Town Hall in March 1988. Professor James
Gaddarn, of Trinity College of Music in London, was gathering
Ealing Choral Society and Orchestra to launch into the profoundly
beautiful notes of the final movement when there was a sudden
crash. A door slammed at the back of the hall and you could have
heard a pin drop.

In the hush Professor Gaddarn, who had his back to the audience,
felt a prickle of anxiety. 'I heard this commotion. It was like a horse
coming down the aisle. I heard footsteps behind me coming towards
the rostrum.'

He turned round and there was this apparition: a spaceman in
glittering, silver helmet, black leggings, chains, heavy gauntlets and
big boots.

'What on earth do you want?' hissed the professor. Mumble,
mumble, said the spaceman, but the professor was unable to understand a word. 'It eventually tumbled out that he was from a kisso-
gram agency. By quick cross-examination I was able to discover
that he had come to the wrong hall.'

Clank, clank. Away clumped the spaceman. The professor raised
his baton and completed the enjoyable work.

THE WORST MUSIC CRITIC

Any critic can fail to spot a genius, but only James William Davison
had the daunting consistency to miss every single one for an entire
century. The great man was editor of *Musical World* magazine
(1843–80) in London and his every pronouncement has now been
proved wrong by posterity.

In his stimulating career he dismissed Tchaikovsky's *Romeo and
Juliet* as 'rubbishy', said that Verdi's *Rigoletto* would 'flicker and flare

for a night or two and then be forgotten', and argued that 'Wagner cannot write music'. He slated *Tannhauser* as 'commonplace, lumbering and awkward', *The Flying Dutchman* as 'hideous' and *Lohengrin* as 'an incoherent mass of rubbish'. He felt that Liszt was 'talentless funghi', Berlioz was 'more a vulgar lunatic than a healthy musician', and Schumann's entire output was so devoid of melody or form that it 'can hardly be called music at all'.

Schubert got a complete pasting, being 'overrated and literally beneath criticism'. The great critic also felt that Chopin was 'knotty, crude and ill-digested'. His entire works present 'a motley surface of ranting hyperbole and excruciating cacophony' full of clumsy harmonies, sickly melodies and an utter ignorance of design which 'wholly forbid the possibility of Chopin being a skilled or even moderately proficient artist'.

In the whole nineteenth-century scene Davison could detect only one unquestioned genius who would become a household name: Mr Sterndale Bennet. When others scoffed at this choice, the unshakeable critic said: 'Let posterity award to each his real deserts.'

TWELVE

THE SPIRIT OF THE OLYMPICS

In which the human body is pushed to its limits, slipping, falling, almost drowning and starting fights on a banana boat.

MARATHONS CAN BE FUN

In 1966 Shizo Kanakuri set a new record for the Olympic marathon. At Stockholm he completed the 26·2-mile course in an unbeatable 54 years, 8 months, 6 days, 8 hours, 32 minutes and 20.3 seconds, having started in 1912.

He had run several miles before passing a group of people having a very pleasant drink in their front garden. As he was suffering from chronic heat exhaustion at the time he did the only sensible thing and tottered over to join them. Being a sociable sort of man, he stayed for a few more drinks whereupon he changed his race tactics dramatically, caught a train back to Stockholm, booked into a hotel for the night, boarded the next boat to Japan, got married, had six children and ten grandchildren, before returning to the villa where he had stopped and completing the marathon for the honour of Japan.

THE LEAST SUCCESSFUL NATIONAL TEAM AT THE OLYMPICS

In 1932 the Olympic Games sent its first-ever invitation to China, reckoning that its population of 500 million people must contain one person interested in athletics. And so it turned out.

A letter of acceptance came, saying that China would be represented, and this was followed by complete silence until Mr Cheung-Chun-Liu arrived out of the blue at the Los Angeles Olympic village on 27 July. Speaking not one word of English, he eventually managed to convey through an interpreter that he was, in fact, the entire Chinese Olympic team.

Three days later all eyes were on Mr Liu as he took part in the preliminary heats of the 100 and 200 metres, pitted against the three finest sprinters in the world. He was on the track 40 seconds in total, came a resounding last in both heats and went straight back to China.

THE LEAST SUCCESSFUL HERO'S RETURN

At the 1932 Olympics in Los Angeles, Santiago Alberto Lovell won a gold medal for heavyweight boxing, which is no concern of ours.

Lovell redeemed the situation, however, on the boat trip home. So bad was the food on board that the team appointed him to be their spokesman with the captain. When the protest got nowhere, he led what was later described as 'a mutiny' in which fighting broke out. Unbiased onlookers said the Argentinians did some of their best boxing for years in these moments, but the captain called an armed guard who kept the Olympic team under lock and key for the rest of the voyage.

Instead of the predictable hero's welcome at Buenos Aires Docks, Lovell was named as the ringleader, surrounded by armed police and carted off to jail in handcuffs.

WORST PENTATHLON TEAM

Only Tunisia has really explored the possibilities of modern pentathlon, in which athletes show quite unnecessary prowess in five different sports.

At the 1960 Rome Olympics they scored no points at all in the riding event because the entire team fell off their horses. It was the first time that anyone had scored nought at the Olympics.

Encouraged by this start, they hit sizzling form in the swimming, where one of their people nearly drowned and the versatile Ennachi (who had already fallen off a horse) took twice as long to complete a mere 300 metres as the winner. Their shooting was described as 'wild' and they were ordered from the range because they were endangering the lives of the judges.

When it came to the fencing, only one of their team could do it, so they kept sending the same man out. During the third bout his

opponent said 'I've fought you before', ripped off his visor and had him disqualified.

Tunisia came a splendid seventeenth out of seventeen. They were a spectacular 9,000 points behind the leaders and scored half as many as Germany who came sixteenth. It is the lowest-ever pentathlon score and an example to us all.

SLOWEST OLYMPIC ATHLETE

At the 1976 Olympics in Montreal, Olmeus Charles from Haiti was last by the largest margin ever recorded. He set an all-time record for the 10,000 metres race. Giving the crowd tremendous value for money, he completed the course in 42 minutes 00.11 seconds. Everyone lapped him at least three times and the winner finished so far ahead he would have had time to complete another 5,000 metres.

An argument broke out among the track officials as to whether he should be allowed to finish the course. Happily, the crowd were not denied this fine sight and the entire Olympic timetable was held up by fourteen minutes.

SLOWEST START TO AN OLYMPIC HEAT

A relaxing start is, of course, essential to anyone who really wants to enjoy a race. The finest such start was achieved by the American athletes, Eddie Hart and Ray Robinson, who held the 100 metres world record and would not normally interest us. In 1972, however, they pulled out something a little bit extra, missed the bus from the Olympic village and watched their own race on television. This gave them a much fuller overall sense of the whole event.

THE LEAST SUCCESSFUL ATTEMPT TO BREAK AN OLYMPIC RECORD

At the glorious 1932 Olympic Games, the Finnish athlete Iso-Hollo was hot favourite to break the world record for the 3,000 metres steeplechase. Roaring into the lead from the first lap, he was on target for a new time and turned the corner expecting to hear the bell for the final lap.

At this point one of the Olympic all-time greats intervened. The official lap-counter was, in fact, looking the wrong way, being absorbed in the decathlon pole vault nearby. He failed to ring the bell for the last lap and the entire field kept on running.

When he finally got back on the job, Iso-Hollo completed the race in 10 minutes 33.4 seconds. It was the slowest-ever time for the 3,000 metres steeplechase, but then they did run an extra 450 metres.

THE WORST SKI JUMPER

Few people know who won the 90 metres ski jump at the 1988 Winter Olympics in Calgary. Everyone, however, knows that Eddie 'the Eagle' Edwards came a definitive last, flapping both arms for mid-air balance and complaining that he could not see anything because his pebble spectacles steamed up during take-off.

A plasterer from Cheltenham, he amazed everyone by deciding to enter the Olympics after several practice runs on the local dry ski slope.

His fame went before him and a huge, cheering crowd met him at the airport where his plane arrived late and his bag split open so that every piece of his gear went round and round the luggage carousel with Eddie in hot pursuit.

Next morning he found that his ski bindings had been crushed and so he missed his first two practice jumps while they were repaired. He got in one jump and survived only to find that he was locked out of his cabin with all his clothes inside.

When he did get to the press centre, he was not allowed into his own press conference because he did not have the right credentials.

Known as 'the barmy Brit', he soon gained a huge following throughout the world. Millions watched his jump and when he landed he raised his arms in a salute normally reserved for the outright winner.

A living embodiment of the Olympic spirit, he said that he did not train in the gym because it made him ache. He was later invited on to a chat show with Burt Reynolds and driven around his home town in an open-top bus so that ecstatic multitudes could get a glimpse of him.

LEAST SUCCESSFUL OLYMPIC SWIMMER

Carolyn Schuler of the USA won the 100 metres butterfly at the 1960 Rome Olympics in a new world-record time. She was, however, completely overshadowed by her team-mate, Miss Carolyn Wood, who dived into the pool swam one length, turned, disappeared beneath the water and gave every appearance of having become the first swimmer to drown during the Olympic Games.

Miss Wood eventually rose spluttering to the surface and grasped the lane rope, whereupon her coach dived in fully clothed to administer resuscitation. Afterwards she told the eager reporters: 'I got a big mouthful of water and could not go on.'

THIRTEEN

STORIES WE FAILED TO PIN DOWN

In which are gathered stories, unproved and uncertain. But there is no smoke without fire.

THE LEAST APPRECIATED WORK OF ART

In a fine burst of indignation a London art student created a piece of sculpture designed to show man's inhumanity to artists. He spent three days at the Royal Festival Hall arranging the work, which comprised a circle of metal helmets surrounded by pieces of aluminium and graphite.

At the preview 1,000 guests trod all the graphite into the carpet and, before the exhibition opened to the public, conscientious cleaners threw the entire work into the rubbish skip. The artist later said this was 'very significant'.

THE LEAST SUCCESSFUL KAMIKAZE PILOT

During the last world war a Japanese Kamikaze pilot made no less than eleven suicide flights. Although he set off with enough petrol for a one-way trip and no weapons of self-defence and the ritual farewell from his commanding officer, he came back safely each time and went on to write an autobiography in which he claimed that the planes were unsafe.

A member of the Japanese Special Attack Corps, he lived till he was ninety-three.

THE LEAST SUCCESSFUL WITCH

In 1978 a witch put a curse on Nottingham Forest Football Club. In that year they won the League Championship and Football League Cup with the longest unbeaten run in the history of English football before going on to win the European Cup two years in succession.

181

THE LEAST SUCCESSFUL ZOO

In 1972 a husband and wife bought a small zoo in a peaceful village near Bordeaux in south-west France. When they took over it was an ordinary zoo with nothing of interest to our sort of student. It had 300 animals, including 64 bison, the largest collection of hyenas in captivity and enough Brent geese to sate the most avid fan.

Two years later they had 75 animals: bison were thin on the ground, there was only one hyena and that was being treated for a prolapsed uterus and there was not a Brent goose in sight.

The exodus started when six old giraffes moved off, like pensioners going to the country to end their days in peace.

Unlike pensioners, however, they were chased by gendarmes all the way to the coast. After they beat it, the seals did a bunk and one called 'Flipper' was found crossing the Bordeaux-Arcachon highway.

Then all hell broke loose and for some months the town's inhabitants became accustomed to wallabies, hyenas, chimpanzees, giant pumas and all variety of exotic birds roaming the streets.

No zoo-keeper has done more to spread interest in wildlife among the community and, before long, stampedes became a hazard for cyclists.

THE LEAST SUCCESSFUL PURCHASE OF A PET

In 1980 an Italian businessman in Brescia was sent out to buy a pet dog for his children. When he returned with a small fluffy bundle an immediate family argument broke out as to what breed it was. His wife insisted it was a fine-haired chihuahua and his children would not sleep for claiming it was a poodle, while the buyer himself would hear no word against his own belief that it was a pedigree labrador, as the salesman had told him.

Only when they took the animal to the vet after three months,

182

complaining that it never barked, did they learn that it was, in fact, a lion.

NOT SINCE KING ALFRED

King Alfred only scratched the surface of what is possible when baking. In 1987, for example, a lady cottage-dweller in Dartmoor, Devon, popped some scones into the oven and completely forgot about them.

An hour later, just as she was stepping into the bath, she suddenly recalled them. Without even grabbing a towel, she dashed, stark-naked, into the kitchen and was gripping the oven handle when there was a knock on the back door. Knowing that the baker habitually walked in and put bread on the table, she nipped into the broom cupboard.

Hiding in the darkness, she heard the latch click and footsteps crossing the kitchen, whereupon the cupboard door was opened by the gasman who had come to read the meter. 'Oh,' said this fine woman, 'I was expecting the baker.' When she got out, the scones were burned.

THE LEAST SUCCESSFUL TAXI RIDE

The Frankfurt Book Fair is an annual gathering of publishers, noted as much for all-night whoopee-making as for services to literature. In the 1980s a Dutch publisher left his seventh party in three hours and hailed a cab.

Burrowing in his wallet, he pulled out a card bearing the name and address of his Frankfurt hotel before collapsing into restorative sleep on the back seat. Next morning he woke up outside his home in Amsterdam, having shown the wrong card.

THE LEAST SUCCESSFUL SUNBATHER

In 1983 a Californian sunbather decided to acquire the perfect tan. Hearing that a better-quality ray was available above the urban smog, he attached 42 helium balloons to his deckchair which was itself tethered to the earth by means of a long rope.

He was supposed to rise 6,000 feet and there bask in the ultra-violet possibilities. However, he did much better than this when his rope snapped and the deckchair rose, untrammelled, to a height of 15,000 feet, where a passing airline pilot reported him as a UFO sighting.

Prepared for all possibilities, he pulled out an air pistol and shot the balloons one by one. His deckchair demolished a power cable, blacking out the whole area, and he arrived back on earth much paler than when he left.

THE LEAST SUCCESSFUL HUNTER

In 1985 a hunter went duck-shooting in New Zealand. A less fair-minded man would have fired both barrels at the duck, causing unnecessary carnage. With a keen sense of justice, however, our man fired both barrels and missed, whereupon the duck circled round, dive-bombed, knocked him over and shattered his glasses.

THE WORST HAMMER THROWING

At an athletics event in the north-east of England during 1952 a hammer thrower broke all known records. With a superhuman effort he swirled and let go of the hammer which flew out of the enclosure, smashed onto the bonnet of his own Triumph Spitfire that he had arranged to sell that night, causing £150 worth of damage, before bouncing off through the window of the athletics office and knocking out the regional organizer for hammer throwing who had been called away to telephone his wife.

At previous events he had hit an Esso petrol station, a police car and the Gents, from which a cowering spectator had emerged with the belief that he had been struck by lightning.

THE LEAST IDEAL COUPLE

In 1983 a televison company held a nationwide competition to find 'Britain's ideal couple'. The winning pair duly appeared in all the papers, smiling happily and giving extensive interviews about the secret of their successful relationship.

Had it ended there this unseemly bliss would merely have depressed the entire nation. The couple, however, turned out to be far more interesting than anyone would have suspected. The day before the programme was broadcast the young woman announced that their engagement was off because her fiancé had (a) smacked her face at a Lindisfarne concert and (b) kept from her the fact that he was already married to a woman called Barabara who had thought that *they* were the ideal couple. The programme was broadcast as planned.

LEAST SUCCESSFUL DIVERS

In 1979 a West Country sub-aqua club gained permission to dive in Britain's most inaccessible loch. Happy in the knowledge that they were the first-ever people to explore the underwater world of remotest Scotland, they drove 740 miles, climbed 3,000 feet, put on their gear and plunged in to find that it was only four feet deep.

LEAST SUCCESSFUL MOTORCYCLIST

Thrilled with his new purchase in 1981, a would-be motorcyclist in Smyrna, USA, invited his best friend round to see the gleaming machine.

'Want to see how it works?' the proud owner asked.

'Sure, why not?' replied the buddy.

He cranked the engine, which roared into life and the bike shot through sliding glass doors, dragging its owner with it.

The ambulance was called, while his wife mopped up the spilled gasoline with tissue paper and threw it down the lavatory.

When our man returned 'wrapped up like a mummy', according to the local newspaper, he went into the lavatory and, reflecting upon the day, lit a cigarette. When he threw the fag end down the bowl, he was thrown against the door by the resulting explosion.

Finding him on the floor again, his wife decided to call the ambulance once more. As he was carried out, face down, on a stretcher, his wife said 'Never mind, dear, nothing else can go wrong,' whereupon one of the attendants tripped over the motorcycle and our hero fell to the floor, injuring his leg.

At this moment he announced that he was putting the motorbike up for sale without ever riding it.

THE LEAST SUCCESSFUL ATTEMPT TO OPT OUT

Fearing another world war, a Canadian pacifist decided to sell his home and move to a quiet part of the planet where peace was guaranteed. After months of deliberation he chose the remotest and safest spot on the atlas.

In March 1982 he moved to the Falkland Islands, just five days before the Argentinians invaded this quiet island, marking the start of the Falklands war.

THE LEAST EFFECTIVE BIRTH CONTROL CAMPAIGN

After twelve months an Asian birth control conference announced that their recent campaign was 'a complete fiasco'. A subsequent survey showed that 79 per cent of the men had taken the pill and 98 per cent had continued putting the condom on their finger, as they were shown in the demonstration.

Later that year, the Chinese minister for birth control offered to resign when it was announced that the population of his country had increased by 13 million, the equivalent of the entire population of Australia, during his two years in office.

WORST LABOUR RELATIONS CONFERENCE

A conference on 'New Ways of Bringing Harmony to the Work Place' was organized in Stockholm in the late 1970s. It was postponed when the catering union went on strike in support of six electricians who were wrongfully dismissed for working to rule during a pay claim after being asked to do more work without consultation.

LEAST SUCCESSFUL POP RECORDS

During the 1970s a new singing phenomenon brought out three records.

One was called 'I'm a Pirate King' which, before demand slumped, sold eleven copies. 'I was knocked out when I heard,' the performer said. 'It's going to be a great hit.'

He improved upon this when his next single, 'The Cuckoo Clock', sold three copies. His most memorable record, however, was a version of 'Old King Cole' with a heavy synthesizer backing. It sold one copy worldwide.

'I'm going to be a star,' the singer observed. To us, of course, he already is.

THE OVERTURE THAT WENT WITH A BANG

As a special attraction, one of America's symphony orchestras gave a performance of Tchaikovsky's *1812 Overture* with sixteen real cannons. At a critical moment a fault occurred in the electrical firing system and all sixteen went off together activating the smoke alarms.

Even more rousing than usual, the final passage of the overture contained additional fire bells, hooters, several claxons, a shower of safety foam from the sprinklers and the combined sirens of six fire engines which arrived as the auditorium was being evacuated.

THE WORST TULIP FESTIVAL

For decades a town in the Midlands held a tulip festival on May Day which was the highspot of its horticultural year. In 1975 the Labour Party lost control of the council in local elections. The incoming Conservatives felt that the date was far too ideological and moved it two weeks later.

The tulips, however, were not informed and so they flowered as usual and were all over by May 14. The festival went ahead without them, as it was too late to withdraw the advertising.

THE LEAST SUCCESSFUL SLIMMERS

Despite avid enthusiasm and regular attendance no member of a group described as the Sheddit Slimming Circle of Arkansas lost a single pound during its 16-year existence. Indeed, their president was comparatively slender when he took office, but in no time had ballooned to the same roly-poly proportions as his membership.

The Circle was disbanded in 1954 when they were banned by the community centre committee. At an acrimonious meeting the janitor said he was 'tired of cleaning up the mess of cake and cookie crumbs after their sessions'.

THE LEAST SUCCESSFUL CHESS CHALLENGE

In the 1980s a Yugoslavian chess master challenged twenty people to play him simultaneously. He further offered to wear a blindfold.

Having specialized in this form of challenge, he knew that the trick was to keep each game as different as possible so he could distinguish between them. On this occasion, however, the twenty opponents ganged up and agreed to play the same set of pre-arranged moves.

By move five, each had played a more or less random permutation of five moves from a set of eight possibles. Nobody can remember twenty of those.

At this stage the outstanding Yugoslavian produced his shrewdest move: he went to the lavatory and did not return. After breaking down the door they found the window open and footsteps in the snow leading to the railway station.

FOURTEEN

THE ART OF BEING WRONG

Next to being right in this world, the best of all things is to be clearly and definitely wrong.

T. H. Huxley

Being wrong is a human art as old as temple decoration and ball-room dancing. No facet of life has been untouched by this unique capacity.

LITERATURE

'Sentimental rubbish . . . Show me one page that contains an idea' – *Odessa Courier* on *Anna Karenina* by Leo Tolstoy, 1877.

* * * *

'Shakespeare's name, you may depend on it, stands absurdly too high and will go down' – Lord Byron, 1814.

* * * *

'His fame is gone out like a candle in a snuff and his memory will always stink' – William Winstanley, 1687 on Milton.

* * * *

'It is becoming painfully obvious that Henry James has written himself out as far as any kind of novel writing is concerned' – William Morton Payne in 1884, before James had written *The Bostonians*, *The Turn of The Screw*, *The Ambassadors*, *What Maisie Knew*, *The Aspern Papers*, *The Golden Bowl* and most of the novels upon which his reputation now rests.

* * * *

'Monsieur Flaubert is not a writer' – *Le Figaro*, 1857.

* * * *

'Mr Waugh displays none of the *élan* that distinguishes the true satirist' – Dudley Fitts reviewing Evelyn Waugh's *Vile Bodies* in 1930.

* * * *

'A hundred years from now it is very likely that *The Jumping Frog* alone will be remembered' – Harry Thurston Peck on the works of Mark Twain, 1901.

* * * *

'I'm sorry, Mr Kipling, but you just don't know how to use the English language' – The *San Francisco Examiner*'s rejection letter to Rudyard Kipling in 1889.

* * * *

'This is a book of the season only' – *New York Herald Tribune* on *The Great Gatsby* by F. Scott Fitzgerald.

* * * *

'Few are good for much' – Henry Hallam on John Donne's poetry.

* * * *

'We do not believe in the permanence of his reputation ... our children will wonder what their ancestors could have meant by putting Dickens at the head of the novelists of his day" – *Saturday Review*, 1858.

* * * *

'We cannot name one considerable poem of his that is likely to remain upon the thresh-floor of fame' – *London Weekly Review*, 1828 on Samuel Taylor Coleridge.

* * * *

THE ART OF BEING WRONG

'It would be useless to pretend that they can be very widely read' – *Manchester Guardian* on *Youth* and *Heart of Darkness* by Joseph Conrad, 1902.

*   *   *   *

'Chaucer, notwithstanding the praises bestowed upon him ... does not deserve so well as Thomas Erceldoune' – Lord Byron, 1835.

*   *   *   *

'His versification is so destitute of sustained harmony and many of his thoughts are so strained ... that I have always believed his verses would soon rank with forgotten things' – John Quincy Adams on Lord Byron, 1830.

*   *   *   *

'The only consolation which we have in reflecting upon it is that it will never be generally read' – James Lorimer reviewing *Wuthering Heights* by Emily Brontë, 1847.

*   *   *   *

'Monsieur de Balzac's place in French literature will be neither considerable nor high' – Eugene Poitou in the *Review des Deux Mondes*, 1856.

*   *   *   *

'In a hundred years time the histories of French literature will only mention it as a curio' – Emile Zola on *Les Fleurs Du Mal* by Charles Baudelaire, 1857.

*   *   *   *

'An endless wilderness of dull, flat, prosaic twaddle' – T. B. Macauley on *The Prelude* by William Wordsworth.

* * * *

'Nothing odd will do long. *Tristram Shandy* did not last' – Samuel Johnson in 1776 on a novel that is still in print 212 years later.

* * * *

'My dear fellow, I may perhaps be dead from the neck up, but rack my brains as I may I can't see why a chap should need thirty pages to describe how he turns over in bed before going to sleep' – Marc Humbolt, a French editor, rejecting *In Remembrance of Times Past* by Marcel Proust in 1912.

MUSIC

'I would say that this does not belong to the art which I am in the habit of considering music' – A. Oulibicheff reviewing Beethoven's *Fifth Symphony*.

* * * *

'As a work of art, it is naught' – The *New York Times* review of Bizet's *Carmen*, 24 October 1878.

* * * *

'Not only does Monsieur Berlioz not have any melodic ideas, but, when one occurs to him, he does not know how to handle it, for he does not know how to write' – P. Scudo, *Critique et Litterature Musicales*, 1852.

* * * *

THE ART OF BEING WRONG

'The art of composing without ideas has decidedly found in Brahms one of its worthiest representatives' – Hugo Wolf, 1886.

* * * *

'Had he submitted this music to a teacher, the latter, it is to be hoped, would have torn it up and thrown it at his feet' – L. Rellstab reviewing Chopin's *Mazurkas* in 1833.

* * * *

'Debussy's music is the dreariest kind of rubbish' – *New York Post*, 22 March 1907.

* * * *

'Liszt is a mere commonplace person with his hair on end. He writes the ugliest music extant' – *Dramatic and Musical Review*, London, 1843.

* * * *

'It is not fair to the readers of the *Musical Courier* to take up their time with a detailed description of that musical monstrosity, which masquerades under the title of Gustav Mahler's *Fourth Symphony*. There is nothing in the design, content, or execution of the work to impress the musician' – *Musical Courier*, New York, 9 November 1904.

* * * *

'Devoid of all musical interest' – *New York World* on Prokofiev, 21 November 1918.

* * * *

'Silly and inconsequential' – H. E. Krehbiel reviewing Puccini's *La Bohème* in the *New York Tribune*, 27 December 1900.

* * * *

'Ravel's *Bolero* I submit as the most insolent monstrosity ever perpetrated in the history of music' – Edward Robinson, *The American Mercury*, May 1932.

* * * *

'The harmonies are so obtrusively crude that no number of wrong notes would be detected by the subtlest listeners' – H. F. Chorley, on Schumann's *Variations for Two Pianofortes*.

* * * *

'Vulgar, self-indulgent and provincial beyond all description' – Virgil Thomson on Sibelius' Second Symphony in the *New York Herald Tribune*, 11 October 1940.

* * * *

'Strauss can be characterized in four words: little talent, much impudence' – Cesar Cui, 5 December 1904.

* * * *

'It is probable that much, if not most, of Stravinsky's music will enjoy brief existence' – W. J. Henderson, *New York Sun*, 16 January 1937.

* * * *

'Tchaikovsky's First Piano Concerto, like the first pancake, is a flop' – Nicolai Soloviev, *Novoye Vremya*, St Petersburg, 13 November 1875.

* * * *

'As an opera, *Eugene Onegin* is stillborn and absolutely incompetent' – Cesar Cui, *Nedelya*, St Petersburg, 5 November 1884.

* * * *

'*Rigoletto* is the weakest work of Verdi. It lacks melody. This opera has hardly any chance of being kept in the repertoire' – *Gazette Musicale de Paris*, 22 May 1853.

* * * *

'I scarcely think it will be able to keep the stage for any length of time' – E. A. Kelley, reviewing Wagner's *Lohengrin*, 2 April 1854.

* * * *

'The musical value of this score is precisely zero' – *Echo*, Berlin No. 22, reviewing Wagner's opera *Rienzi* in 1871.

* * * *

'But oh, the pages of stupid and hopelessly vulgar music! The unspeakable cheapness of the chief tune. ... Do you believe way down in the bottom of your heart that if this music had been written by Mr John L. Tarbox, now living in Sandown, New Hampshire, any conductor here or in Europe could be persuaded to put it in rehearsal?' – Philip Hale on Beethoven's Ninth Symphony in the *Musical Record*, Boston, 1 June 1899.

* * * *

'Brahms evidently lacks the breadth and power of invention eminently necessary for the production of truly great symphonic work' – *Musical Courier*, New York, 1887.

* * * *

'Who has heard THAT, and finds it beautiful, is beyond help' – Eduard Hanslick on Liszt's B-minor Sonata, 1881.

* * * *

'Beethoven always sounds to me like the upsetting of bags of nails, with here and there an also dropped hammer' – John Ruskin, 6 February 1881.

* * * *

'Sure-fire rubbish' – Lawrence Gilman reviewing *Porgy and Bess* by George Gershwin in the *New York Herald Tribune*, 1935.

* * * *

'The Beatles? They're on the wane' – the Duke of Edinburgh in Canada in 1965. They went on to produce five albums and eleven singles most of which got to number one.

EVERYTHING ELSE

'And for the tourist who really wants to get away from it all – safaris in Vietnam' – *Newsweek* predicting popular holidays for the late 1960s.

* * * *

'Sterility may be inherited' – *Pacific Rural News*.

* * * *

'The Olympic Games can no more have a deficit than a man can have a baby' – Mayor Jean Drapeau of Montreal three weeks before the 1976 Olympics as a result of which his city lost one billion dollars.

* * * *

THE ART OF BEING WRONG

'ALL THE PASSENGERS ARE SAFE' – *Lancashire Evening Post* headline on their report of the *Titanic* sinking.

* * * *

'DEWEY DEFEATS TRUMAN' – *Chicago Tribune* headline on 4 November 1948 after the convincing re-election of President Truman to office.

* * * *

'Television won't last. It's a flash in the pan' – Mary Somerville, pioneer of radio educational broadcasts, 1948.

* * * *

'If the Earth did move at tremendous speed, how could we keep a grip on it with our feet? We could walk only very, very slowly; and should find it slipping rapidly under our footsteps. Then, which way is it turning? If we walked in the direction of its tremendous speed, it would push us on terribly rapidly. But if we tried to walk against its revolving . . . ? Either way we should be terribly giddy, and our digestive process impossible' – Margaret Missen, *The Sun Goes Round The Earth*.

* * * *

'You care for nothing but shooting dogs and rat-catching and you will be a disgrace to yourself and all your family' – Charles Darwin's father reviewing his son's academic and career prospects.

* * * *

'The Moon has a coating of ice 140 miles thick' – Hans Horbiger, author of *World Ice Theory*.

* * * *

'Everything that can be invented has been invented' – the Director of the US Patent Office in 1899.

* * * *

'Unworthy of the attention of practical or scientific men' – the conclusion of a Parliamentary Committee's report on whether Edison's electric light bulb would ever be relevant to Britain.

* * * *

'Democracy will be dead by 1950' – John Langdon-Davies, *A Short History of The Future*, 1936.

* * * *

'There is no likelihood man can ever tap the power of the atom' – Dr Robert Mullikan, 1923 Nobel Prize winner.

* * * *

'In all likelihood world inflation is over' – Managing Director of the International Monetary Fund, 1959.

* * * *

'Very interesting, Whittle, my boy, but it will never work' – The Professor of Aeronautical Engineering at Cambridge University when shown Frank Whittle's plan for the jet engine.

* * * *

'I make bold to say that I don't believe that in the future history of the world any such feat will be performed by anybody else' – the Mayor of Dover in 1875 after Matthew Webb had swum the English channel.

LORD KELVIN : A SPECIAL TRIBUTE

'Radio has no future' – Lord Kelvin, President of the Royal Society, 1890–95.

* * * *

'Heavier than air flying machines are impossible' – Lord Kelvin, President of the Royal Society, 1890–95.

* * * *

'X-rays will prove to be a hoax' – Lord Kelvin, President of the Royal Society, 1890–95.

AND, OF COURSE

This book was specially written to mark the tenth anniversary of *The Book of Heroic Failures*.

Only when the festivities were in full swing, celebrating a splendid decade, did the author notice that the original book in fact came out nine years ago.

Mr Pile said, 'I don't know how it happened.'